THE BACKPACK

A Wounded Police Officer's Struggle with the Burden All Cops Share

by Brandon Hultink

Quill
Driver
Books

Fresno, California

Published by Quill Driver Books
An imprint of Linden Publishing
2006 South Mary Street, Fresno, California 93721
(559) 233-6633 / (800) 345-4447
QuillDriverBooks.com

Quill Driver Books and Colophon are trademarks of
Linden Publishing, Inc.
ISBN 978-1-61035-351-9

135798642

Printed in the United States of America on acid-free paper.

Library of Congress Cataloging-in-Publication Data on file.

DEDICATION

To Heff, a "cop's cop," who helped me through the storm.

To Jordan and Zac, whose smiling faces in the dark got me through it.

To Cody, truly my "miracle son!"

To Mom and Dad Hultink, who gave me the place to write and the encouragement to finish.

To JJ, who held my hand when I needed it most.

To all my family and loved ones, for giving me the strength to see tomorrow.

To all my brothers and sisters under the badge for all you do each day: be safe.

To Keri, my rock and the love of my life, thank you for carrying me when I could not walk.

I love you all and cherish each day with you. May God bless you all.

—Brandon

CONTENTS

INTRODUCTION

It has taken me over fifteen years to begin putting these thoughts down as words on paper. There are many reasons, but the main one is the very reason this book needed to be written: cops don't talk about their feelings about anything, ever. That is one of the biggest challenges facing every young police officer new to this profession. We see the worst of humanity, shift after shift, and refuse to process the trauma that pounds away at each of us relentlessly. We are the toughest of the tough when we exit our academies and first don the uniform. We start a career of showing each other as officers that each day, each week, and each year we are still tough enough to do the job. We spend our entire career showing how all the madness that we face daily does not affect us in any way. We believe we must show that we are robots of steel—ready at the drop of a hat to face the next mess to which we are called. Meanwhile, as we keep up our façade of invincibility, our core is breaking. We return home daily to the question "How was your day?" and simply answer "Fine" as we pour our first of many post-shift drinks. We refuse to let people outside our police community in, as day by day our strong exterior hides our crumbling inside.

The aftermath is devastating: divorce, suicide, substance abuse, domestic violence, depression, loneliness, and declining overall health. We start out as Spartan warriors fresh out of the academy and turn into shells of ourselves. But the dirty secret in police work is that nobody knows any of this is happening until it's often too late to reverse the destructive course we've set for ourselves. Why? Why do police officers, most of them very skilled, intelligent people, allow themselves to become so self-destructive when their whole lives are devoted to solving other people's problems? I didn't understand it when it was happening to me, and nobody told me about any of this when I was in the police academy.

The reason is so simple it almost defies logic: *police officers will not discuss their feelings and emotions.* Instead, they take the trauma and problems they face during their shifts and stuff these in "the backpack" that they each carry. Nobody on the job ever tells you this, but the things we refuse to process emotionally as police officers, and stuff into our backpacks, will have to be dealt with at some point. Each year we work as an officer, we see the worst parts of humanity that no person should have to see and add that to the weight of our backpack. Each time we end a shift in which a child was decapitated in a car accident or a teenager was raped and murdered and return home to answer "I'm fine" to our spouse or companion, we add to the backpack.

The heavier it gets and the longer we are on the job, the more difficult it becomes to process what has happened to us. So, we turn to self-medication and isolation and share the few feelings we can only with fellow officers "who understand us." These fellow officers are carrying their own backpacks and facing the same mountains each of us is climbing. Officers get together in bars, tell stories, and brag about how tough they were in the face of hundreds of calls; that's only a bandage on a growing wound.

Which brings me to this book. I have fought the urge to write this book for the same reasons I shoved a career of police work into my own backpack. But with the help and advice of many people both inside and outside the police world, I am still alive today to tell this story. This story needs to be told, but only if it can be told so that a police officer will truly understand it. This is my journey through a career in law enforcement, from the academy to the present. I will not hold back. I will let you inside a world that you have not been able to experience before and that will likely make you feel very uncomfortable at times. I am going to open myself up to you by telling you how my backpack was filled and how it affected me. I will let you know how I feel about a lot of things. I will expose the side of police work that people don't see and what officers face daily. I've lost too many friends to suicide, poor health, and destructive behavior in the last several years, and I need to open this wound that each officer is facing. It's time to unzip my backpack.

1

DESPERATION

I can still remember the taste of metal in my mouth from the barrel of the gun. It was just after two o'clock in the morning, and everyone was asleep upstairs. I kept my finger off the trigger, as I had been trained to do my entire career. But I didn't remove the barrel either. I just kept it in my mouth, feeling very lonely and tired. I remember my thoughts drifting to how my whole life I'd been taught that suicide was a one-way ticket to hell. I pictured the devil and an eternity of fire on the "other side" waiting for me as soon as I pulled the trigger. It had been just over six months since I had been shot, and I was paralyzed from the waist down. Just a few months ago I was competing in triathlon races and starting to do well. I can still remember the feeling of running with the wind in my face, looking at my Ironman watch, and challenging myself with each practice run. I remember the mountain-bike trails and endless obstacles each trail posed as my bike cut through the woods. Tears began to well in my eyes as I realized I would never mountain bike or run again. I was now a cripple for life and I'd better accept it, or so I kept being told.

What scared me is how I didn't want to take the gun out of my mouth. I wanted the pain to be over and felt this heavy cloud of hopelessness covering me. My mind flashed to the shooting, and I wondered what I could have done differently. Nothing. Just thinking about the shooting made my side pulse with waves of pain, pain that only the fentanyl was able to dull. It was so quiet in the house that I could actually hear the clock ticking, ticking away time I had looked forward to six months ago. But now, now I couldn't even control my own bowels. Tears were streaming down my face as I shifted the gun in my mouth. I just wanted all of this to be over.

My thoughts shifted to my entire family. To Keri and the boys, to my mom and dad, my brothers and sister, my cousin JJ, my Canadian family, and all my brothers and sisters in blue. I knew there were literally hundreds of people who genuinely cared for me and who would miss me if I were gone. Then the overwhelming feeling of hopelessness cascaded back over me. I knew I'd be a burden to all of these people, and it would be better if I just weren't here. I moved my finger onto the edge of the trigger. I was lying in the hospital bed that they had moved into the house for me. I stubbornly refused to do my lengthy rehab in an inpatient hospital, so they moved the bed into the main floor of our house and scheduled the rehab there. As I lay in the bed, my head faced the wall with the television, which was off. It was dark in the room except for the sliver of light that was hitting this wall between the blinds.

As tears streamed down my face, I had made my mind up to no longer be the burden I felt I was going to be. I had no reason to live as a cripple, and as a thirty-year-old man, I thought my life had been a good run. My finger was now on the trigger, off the trigger guard. I had made up my mind. Then I saw the pictures. They were eight-by-ten-inch pictures of each of my two sons, Jordan and Zachary. Jordan was three and Zachary was just two. They were both smiling. With tears still streaming down my face, I just stared at the pictures. What would my boys say? Were they even old enough to understand? What was I leaving to Keri? All these thoughts were forcing their way to the front of my mind.

Again came the overwhelming feeling of hopelessness. I did not want to be the father who is nothing but a burden to his children. I'll be doing everyone a favor if I just pull the trigger. I closed my eyes and resigned myself to ending it. I remember making sure the barrel was not pointed toward the top of my head, so that the bullet wouldn't exit toward where Keri and the boys were sleeping. Where Keri and the boys were sleeping? Oh my God, what the hell was I thinking? Keri was going to hear the shot, and I knew what she would find. I had been to so many suicide calls that I had lost count. The aftermath of any suicide was such an empty, lonely, and depressing feeling. There were always so many questions from those left behind, and a range of emotions from sadness to anger to confusion.

I wanted the pain to be over so badly. But I couldn't take my eyes off the pictures of the boys. I had never felt so alone in my life and wanted to just end everything. I took the gun out of my mouth, rested it on my chest, and cried for what seemed like hours.

2

THE ACADEMY

I was born and raised in Grand Rapids, Michigan, the oldest of five siblings: brothers Todd, Chad, and Marc, and my only little sister, Tara. I came from a very stable and loving home, raised by my mom and dad, Jane and Bert Hultink. Bert was an immigrant who came from the Netherlands at the age of five. He and his four brothers immigrated with my grandparents to Canada, settling in Wellandport, Ontario. They had a stable home, but it was a hard life, working on area farms as they struggled to get a footing in their new country. After high school, my dad decided to further his education at Calvin College in Grand Rapids, Michigan, and there met my mom, a cute, blond nursing student from California. They made a strikingly handsome couple and married within a few years, settling down in Grand Rapids and making it their home.

On June 4, 1970, I came into the world as Brandon Scott Hultink. My early childhood memories are full of sports and running all over the neighborhood on Griswold Street. I look at kids today with their fixation on cell phones and sadly realize that the incredible childhood I experienced outdoors with all my friends is likely a thing of the past. It was an amazing time of discovery, filled with tree forts and pickup games. There seemed no end to the activities we would invent. We didn't have a lot of money during those years, as my dad was in law school and there were a lot of hungry mouths to feed. I still smile remembering how my mom would iron patches onto our jeans, because we wore so many holes through them. I dearly love my parents for the childhood they gave us, and would change nothing if I could go back.

High school was an awkward time for me, as it is for most of us in different ways. I tried to play most sports but was really good at only a few. I had a lot of friends but battled acne and had bouts of low self-esteem. I was an average "C" student, an under-achiever. I just never seemed to get a confident foothold on who I was in high school, and as a result I just sort of sleepwalked my way through it. One minute I was at a party hanging out with the cool crowd and the next I was standing on the side in the school halls feeling awkward again. I've often said that I wish I could go back to high school with the knowledge and confidence I have now.

Because of my lack of focus in high school, I really never had any goals. I thought about joining the military and gave some consideration to becoming a Marine. I remember visiting a recruiter at age sixteen, and he just smiled and told me to come back in a few years. I certainly never considered becoming a police officer. It simply was never on my radar then. In fact, my life was really heading in the opposite direction. I drank at parties and was already addicted to cigarettes. I tried marijuana a few times, but it made me feel tired, so I didn't make it a habit. Thankfully, that was the only drug I was ever introduced to during my teenage years. I was working odd jobs to keep up the junker cars I was driving. As the end of my senior year approached, I was clueless about what direction my life was taking. While all my friends worked hard to prepare themselves for college and were getting their acceptance letters, I was trying to figure out whether to join the military or get a more serious full-time job. The strain of my unpreparedness was not lost on my parents and made life increasingly difficult at home. Something had to give.

After graduation, I decided to spend the summer in Canada with my favorite cousin Jason, or JJ. My uncle Gerrit and aunt Kathy graciously took me in as I worked full-time for the family book business. It was manual labor in the warehouses, a lot of stacking and restacking books, but I loved being there with JJ and my Canadian family. Not having a clue what I wanted to do, I thought maybe I'd just stay and work on books for the rest of my life. It was steady work and I always ended the day feeling like I had accomplished something.

At the end of the summer, I came home for a few weeks with every intention of returning to Canada to work. But I never returned. For whatever reason I decided to enroll in the local Grand Rapids Junior College and take a couple of general education classes. I wore my hair down to my shoulders, like a hockey player, and didn't really expect to like college any more than I had high school. At first I was right. Zoology and English 101 didn't exactly make me want to stay in school or give me any idea what direction my life should take. But fate took an interesting twist in a drastic way about halfway through my first semester.

I remember walking down the very crowded hallway in between classes and bumping squarely into what felt like a wall. Facing me was this guy with hair as long as mine and a towering frame of well over six feet. He stuck his hand out to shake mine and said, "Mark London, what's your major?" I was surprised by how direct he was but answered, "I'm Brandon Hultink, and it's general ed." He just smiled, handed me his card, and said, "Stop by my office this week. I need to run something by you that you might be interested in." I told him I would, and he was gone. I looked down at his card: "Mark London–Director–Grand Rapids Junior College Police Academy." I had never seen this guy, nor was I interested in joining the police academy. I had seen the academy students in my general ed classes wearing their uniforms and sitting up in their seats as if any moment they might be called to some emergency. That made me smile as I stuffed the card into my pocket and went to class. I didn't stop thinking about what he wanted, though, and was genuinely curious. So I finally went to see him.

Mark London's office was, as indicated on his card, at the school's Police Academy. There were several students in their blue uniform shirts bearing the academy insignia above the right breast pocket. They all looked so confident and every one of them looked me in the eye and said "Hello" or "Good morning." I found it a little unnerving. Immediately recognizable was Mr. London: I heard his booming voice laughing with one of his colleagues. He recognized me and waved me into his office. He again shook hands, smiling, and shocked me when he asked, "So Brandon, you decided to stop by and see what the hell I was talking about?" I couldn't believe that in a passing conversation this guy remembered my name. I couldn't remember people's names I knew, let alone those of people I'd had only a quick conversation with in the hallway. I was curious and figured I was either in trouble for something or, well, I just didn't have a clue. So, sitting across from a guy I barely knew, I began a conversation that would change my life.

He started by asking me a simple question: "Brandon, what goals do you have for yourself looking ahead at the next five years?" My mind went totally blank. Goals? Five years? I wasn't prepared to handle a question like this with any honesty and answered, "I really don't have any. I haven't thought about my life much that far ahead. I guess I want to meet a nice girl and have a steady job doing something I like." As I said the words I could hear myself and how hollow and vanilla they all sounded. He asked me if I had a police record, any arrests. No, somehow I had been fortunate enough to avoid that so far. Then he looked me in the eye and asked, "Have you ever thought about being a cop?" I laughed and said, "Like what, in a uniform with a badge and gun?" "Yes, with a badge and gun if you're assigned to a patrol division, or a suit if in another division, or even plainclothes sometimes." He added, "Brandon, I've got an opportunity for you that is not an easy one but will at least answer the question whether you want to think about becoming a cop or not." "Okay," I said, "what's this big mystery?"

I couldn't believe what he was telling me after that. Here I was, this eighteen-year-old kid fresh out of high school, and this guy was offering to have me sworn in as a deputy in two counties as an undercover officer working in factories in both Lowell and Hudsonville, Michigan. An undercover officer?! Yes. He indicated that I would report to the police chief in those respective cities and work undercover as a general laborer in the factories. I would apply to work in the factories, and once I started working there, I would get to know the employees and see if anyone eventually offered me drugs to buy. This was not going to be a quick assignment and might take up to a year. As Mr. London put it, if after a year nothing illegal had happened, then we'd terminate the assignment. He added that no gun or badge would be given to me, and I'd report to the police chiefs if I was offered drugs. They would then get me some "buy money" to purchase the drugs, using proper undercover protocol. Wow, just like that my life had the opportunity to completely change.

Mr. London told me the assignments would not be easy, as the factory work was monotonous hard labor with long days. Since I was going to be working for two factories I would be working two shifts a day, at least five days a week. He said that I'd receive the pay just as an employee would and that I could keep it. Then I stopped the conversation short and asked him the obvious question: "Why me?" He smiled and waved his hand toward his office window, to the adjacent room where a half-dozen academy students worked. "Look at them," he said. "They all look the same: short military-style hair and the attitude to match." I saw where he was going. He went on, "I needed to find someone who would fit in a factory and, if there is illegal activity going on, would be someone who might be approached." I don't know what that said for my general appearance, but I got the point that I fit in. He added that I would be discouraged from attending college during the assignment, as I'd likely be too tired, and it might expose my cover. Then he added, "But if you complete these assignments in the factories for me, I will put you into the Police Academy. Based on your high school grades, you would never have the opportunity to be accepted into the academy, but based on your contribution to law enforcement I can give you a waiver and grant you admission."

I was stunned by the offer and knew its value instantly. I had squandered my high school years and was barely accepted into the junior college, even with a required probationary period. He started to tell me to take a few days and think about it, but I interrupted him. "I'll do it. Let's set this up with the police chiefs." We shook hands and just like that I started a career in police work.

My experiences with the Hudsonville and Lowell police chiefs were very different, but the result was the same. First, they swore me in as a deputy sheriff in both Kent and Ottawa Counties. I was given police identifications for each agency and instructed not to carry them on me when I went to work. Then I spent the day training on how to handle various situations involving the buying or selling of drugs. I was not to use drugs, and if I were pressured to use, I was to simply tell the person I had to "drop" for my probation officer that week and couldn't. Finally, we discussed how to contact the police chiefs and how often. I was to use my undercover name only when applying and working at the factories. I was now known as Cody Miller. Smiling, I left my second police chief's meeting and drove home, still not sure how I had gotten myself into this mess.

The application process was actually pretty easy. Each factory hired me almost on the spot for full-time work, mainly because, I think, I was a high school graduate. But I honestly looked the part: long hair, three-day beard, and still fairly rough callused hands from the work in the book warehouse all summer. At the first factory I was assigned to a machine that I will never forget: the metal ring stamper. At the pace of over ten metal rings a minute I was expected to stamp the ring, grab a new one, oil it, and stamp it. This was the most mind-numbing work I have ever encountered before or since. Quite frankly, that machine drove me to study hard in college after I completed my assignment. I knew after months with this machine that I never wanted to work in a factory again. I also knew I deserved nothing more than to work in a factory after the way I had shunned studying and squandered my high-school years. But this new opportunity brought me hope and I wasn't about to screw it up.

I found myself working these jobs almost on autopilot. I rarely showered, I smoked more than two packs of cigarettes a day, and I slept all weekend just to recover from the week's work. This work continued week after week, month after month. I made friends in each factory, but both police chiefs were getting more anxious about my lack of progress. They indicated they were getting information that drugs were being sold rampantly in both factories. So far, all I'd seen was some of the employees smoking marijuana on their breaks. After about the sixth month, I was in one of the break rooms having a cigarette, and the foreman came into the room and sat down. He told me he was happy with my work but saw how tired I looked. I told him I had two kids and needed to work two jobs to support them. He laughed and said he knew how it was. We talked about fishing for a while, and he asked me if I'd ever used a pick-me-up to get through the day. I asked him if he meant no-doze pills you get at the gas station. He said no, something better, as he slid a small, square, white mini-zip toward me. He told me that this one was free, I should try a little at a time by snorting it, and I'd be able to work nonstop without feeling tired. He told me to come only to him if I needed more and to keep it between us, but said lots of people working in the factory used a pick-me-up to get through the long days.

I turned the powder over to the police chief, and it tested positive for cocaine. I was then able to purchase cocaine from the foreman. After about seven months the investigation in that factory concluded with a successful arrest and ultimate prosecution. In the other factory, after about eight months one of the afternoon-shift managers started selling me marijuana that he obtained somewhere in Grand Rapids. This too led to a successful investigation and prosecution. I had never worked so hard in any job in my whole life, and with the academy acceptance in front of me, I was looking forward to going to school and getting away from the dreaded metal ring stamper.

Mark London was a man of his word and granted my admission to the Police Academy for the 1989 class. After a long-overdue but dreaded haircut, I reported to my first class, Patrol Operations 101, and immediately recognized a friend from high school, Ron Gates. Ron had the frame of a football player and the smile of a charming card dealer. He was well liked by his classmates and loved everything about becoming a cop, including the academy.

From that first class on I followed Ron's lead and took school seriously, immersing myself in every aspect of academy training. With each subject, I was increasingly fascinated with police work as a profession, and by the second year I could actually picture myself in uniform.

Strangely, the undercover work in the factories never really made me feel like I was a police officer. If anything, it felt just the opposite, as I worked day after day at a job I hated with other people who hated it too. It's no wonder they were tempted to do drugs, as I might have been too in similar circumstances.

But something in me was changing. I liked having shorter hair and carried myself with more confidence. I stood straighter and looked people in the eye when I shook hands with them. My parents commented more than once that I was a changed person—for the better. As I neared the completion of the academy, I was ready to become a certified and accredited police officer in the state of Michigan.

During our last year of school, both Ron and I had been working as police cadets for the Grand Rapids Police Department (GRPD). This was my first up-close exposure to police work, and it was an exciting time for both of us. We worked the front desk and took general police reports from citizens who had been in an accident or victims of crime. We occasionally got to ride along with officers and learned quickly that police work was primarily a lot of paperwork and that most of the excitement was simply movie and television exaggeration. Still, I knew that what excitement there was happened out on the streets and not in the police lobby. We couldn't wait to get started.

3

GETTING STARTED

I graduated from the Police Academy in 1990 and passed the state of Michigan officer-certification tests with flying colors. The only thing left was finding a job, and I was applying everywhere. Ron and I were sharing an apartment with two other friends from high school, Kevin Mulder and David Faber. We had endlessly bored them with our plans to apply to and work for the Miami, Detroit, or Honolulu Police Department. We had big dreams, and because neither of us had a steady girlfriend, we gave these dreams some serious consideration. I still laugh when I think about what could have happened had Ron and I gone to Honolulu. I'm not sure we even got as far as applying to any of the departments of our dreams, because instead we stayed a bit closer to home.

Full-time police jobs were very difficult to get in Michigan, and there was competition for every opening. Complicating that was the fact that police jobs nationwide were not plentiful in the 1990s. That left us with one option: work part-time for low pay to gain experience. We did exactly that. Somehow Ron and

I ended up working our first real police job together too, as we were accepted as part-time officers for the Spring Lake/Ferrysburg PD in the summer of 1990. Little did I know it was one of the best cities in Michigan we could ever have worked for.

Starting out meant getting fitted for uniforms. I had some preconceived notions as to how this was going to go. I pictured myself being outfitted with the best and newest uniforms that money could buy, along with all of the recent cutting-edge police equipment. Then the reality of a small police department budget sunk in. Chief Langland fitted us with uniforms from their decades-old supply closet, including an old gun belt and a very old .357 revolver. The uniform hung badly on my thin frame, and I resembled a younger version of Barney Fife. But still, one of the greatest moments in my life occurred when I went out on patrol wearing that uniform, in a police car by myself for the first time. Only rookie police officers can know that feeling, a powerful mixture of pride and uncertainty of what lies ahead, and will never forget their first day on the job.

When I reflect on those first weeks in Spring Lake, I find myself amazed at where and who I was. With the flick of a switch I could force motorists to pull their cars over, whereas twenty-four months before, I was a wayward college student without a clue about what to do with my life. I guess most of us in our early twenties cross the bridge between adolescence and adulthood, but police officers just have to do so faster. Maturity came quickly, as the tremendous weight of responsibility I shouldered each shift became clearer to me. I now carried a gun, and each traffic stop and call for service held the potential for a deadly force decision I might have to make. I might be only twenty years old, but that didn't matter if the dispatcher sent me somewhere. I had to grow up really quickly, whether I ever had to unholster that gun or not.

Thankfully, Spring Lake and Ferrysburg were not as dangerous and busy as were larger Michigan cities. I often look back on my career and wonder how different my life could have been had I stayed in Spring Lake full-time and raised a family there. It is a beautiful community on the edge of Lake Michigan, with a low crime rate and bustling summer vacation atmosphere. Regardless of the time of year, though, most law enforcement was focused on building checks at night and drunk-driving enforcement. Once in a while a drunken driver would fail to stop right away, and a short pursuit would occur, but generally things were pretty quiet. These were the perfect conditions under which to learn the basics of becoming a police officer, without the serious consequences of making the multitude of mistakes a rookie will inevitably make.

After a year of working full-time hours for part-time pay, Ron and I started applying for a job everywhere. We both really wanted to work for the Grand Rapids PD, but the openings just weren't there. We were giving serious consideration to moving to Detroit and working there, but this was not our first preference. Then in the spring of 1991 we both were called for interviews with the Battle Creek Police Department. All I knew about Battle Creek was that cereal was made there, as I had toured the Kellogg's and Post cereal factories in grade school. In law enforcement circles, I had also heard that it was a midsized city with a high crime rate. I was definitely interested in working for a bigger department and looked forward to my interview.

Police interviews in a midsized department like Battle Creek were much different from what I was used to. Up until this point, in nonpolice job situations, I would interview with the boss or possibly a second person such as the manager. However, police interviews are their own animal, and while every department is different, they are not designed to make you feel comfortable. I walked into my Battle Creek PD interview and saw seven people in the room on one side of a large conference table. Three of the interviewers were high-ranking members of the department and in uniform with gold insignia identifying their ranks. One of them I recognized as the chief, from his picture in the lobby. On the other side of the table were a pad of paper and a pen in front of the center chair. Thankfully, instructors at the Grand Rapids Junior College Police Academy had taught us how to handle the various psychological tactics that an interview panel might employ, to give us an edge in maintaining a professional appearance. For starters, I shook hands with each interviewer on the panel, looked each in the eye, and introduced myself.

Then I sat down in the center seat in front of the pad of paper and immediately noticed the seat was very low, making me appear small compared to the panel. Again, prepared for this potential pitfall, I stood up and laughed, stating, "Well, this isn't going to work," as I switched the chair for a taller one to sit on. I had been taught that the panel was assessing whether a candidate would simply accept the poor seating or do something about it, thus exuding a more confident and proactive approach. So, things were off to a good start. After a series of basic questions about myself, the panel members started to increase the difficulty by asking me, "If you were on patrol and pulled the chief of police over on a traffic stop, and subsequently determined he likely had had too much to drink, what would you do?" Tough question, especially with the chief sitting right in front of me. I wasn't ready for the question, but an academy instructor— Eddy Rusticus, a longtime detective—told us if you're interviewing and "get in a pickle," always be yourself and be honest. So I answered, "If I'm being honest, I'd park his car off the road safely and give him a ride home." I followed up, "I realize this is an ethical question, but for me if the question of the chief's sobriety were still in doubt, I'd ask myself whether he might or might not be too intoxicated to drive. I'd make sure he made it home safely. However, if he were in an accident and had harmed anyone, the discretion I might have had to take him home would no longer be available. I'd then run the investigation to its conclusion." I was pretty sure I had screwed that question up by the looks on their faces but found out months later it was one of the best answers they had ever heard. Thank you, Detective Rusticus!

The questions after that seemed easy by comparison. What were my strengths, what were my weaknesses, and why did I want to be a police officer? There were a lot of questions about my experiences at the Spring Lake/Ferrysburg PD, and I was grateful for having the time to comment. All in all, the interview had gone well, but the competition for jobs was fierce and I knew there weren't many openings. Ron and some other academy friends had interviewed with Battle Creek PD as well, and we were hoping to once again land a job together.

On March 25, 1991, Battle Creek police inspector Marylou Belote called and offered me the job that changed everything for me. I was still a twenty-year-old kid, still wet behind the ears, and had no idea what I was in for. Unfortunately, the Battle Creek PD didn't hire Ron, who instead worked some tough years in the Muskegon and Benton Harbor PDs, before he settled into his career with the Kent County Sheriff's Department. I was starting this new journey in Battle Creek completely alone, and I felt it. I was heading to a new city I knew very little about to do a job I knew even less about. Never having served in the military, I imagined it was a lot like standing in the footprints at boot camp and starting a new life with a purpose. But I really didn't have a clue about what would happen to me.

4

"CUB"

After a couple weeks of administrative paperwork and orientation, I was given my official first day on the job: April 8, 1991. I was assigned to my field training officer (FTO), Bill Howe. I couldn't have asked for a better guy to start with. Bill was a day-shift officer with over twenty years' experience. He had a sharp wit and most important knew how to relate to a new guy. Our work together developed into a friendship that continues to this day.

The day shift started at 6:00 a.m., and I remember coming into the locker room for the first time about fifteen minutes before the shift started. It was chaos. I went to my assigned locker, dressed in my uniform, and snapped on my gun belt. The atmosphere was boisterous and I was doing my best to remain unnoticed as I watched men predominantly in their forties joking loudly with each other. One balding officer was wearing the uniform pants of an obviously much larger man and talking about how he had suddenly lost weight, which had everyone laughing. And then he noticed me, and my anonymity was gone.

"Sweet Jesus! What the hell is this? Look, guys, it's a cub, and look how scared he looks! It's okay, cubbie, we'll take care of you," he said sarcastically as he put his arm around me and grinned. He looked at my name tag and went on, "Don't worry, cub, I've taken care of everything for you. Just let Officer Corbin wrap you in his big, strong arms and help you with your fear." He mockingly took out a piece of paper from his front shirt pocket and said, "Look at this letter I got yesterday: 'Dear Officer Corbin, please help our son, Officer Hultink, as he is very afraid in his new police job. He has experienced bed-wetting and night terrors and needs somebody he can look up to who will help him.'"

All the older officers were howling with laughter, and I just stood there with Corbin's arm around me and a stupid grin on my face and just kept my mouth shut. This guy was actually quite funny, and even though it was at my expense, I was glad to be at least introduced to the group in some way instead of feeling quiet and awkward. He went on about how he was going to mentor me and live up to his promise that he "had made to my parents" to protect me. After all of that, we walked up to the lineup room for my first shift briefing.

Growing up I had seen a shift briefing only on the television show *Hill Street Blues*. In a small police department such as Spring Lake/Ferrysburg, a shift briefing does not exist. But at the Battle Creek PD, reality was actually not that far from the TV show. At the front of the room facing about ten officers were three sergeants and a lieutenant. The lieutenant started by introducing the new guys, Officer Jim Mitcavish and me. Then came more jokes about promising my parents to keep me safe and so forth, but the one consistent thing all of them said was "cubbie" or "cub." They didn't call us new officers by name; it was always "cub."

We were being analogized as rookie cops who essentially knew nothing and needed their mama bears for survival. In this new world of bigger-city police work they were right. We were simply cubs, and stumbling and bumbling our way into a big world was going to involve a lot of growing pains. These men were going to be my mama bears, and though they no longer resembled college athletes, I also understood that they knew this job like nobody else. I had a great deal of respect for them already. I was going to follow and watch these guys very closely.

The lineup continued for several minutes, the lieutenant reading off various points of criminal interest, such as suspects in a recent robbery for whom to be on the lookout for, some stolen cars, and their descriptions. After the lieutenant was finished, the shift sergeants each commented briefly on points of interest in their sectors and then released us to start our shifts. We headed outside and got into our patrol cars. After I loaded up our gear, I headed out for my first shift doubled up with Training Officer Howe. The morning air was filled with the smell of Kellogg's and Post cereal, and we headed to the most important stop a police officer makes each day: coffee.

The first order of business for any police officer in Battle Creek at the start of every shift was to immediately drive to Speed's. Speed's had been around forever and had diners in nearly every section of town brewing the best and hottest coffee you could ask for. Beginning a shift without your Speed's coffee was considered a bad start to your day. Once we had our coffees we headed to whatever calls for service the 911 dispatcher gave us. Despite my year with the Spring Lake/Ferrysburg PD, it immediately became clear to me that I knew very little about being a police officer in a bigger city and had much to learn. Officer Howe had an assignment working the north side of

Battle Creek, and as we drove the streets during the shift I saw a mixture of middle-class and economically depressed housing.

During the first four weeks of FTO training, Officer Howe pointed out the basics in various parts of town that would help me when I started working on my own. We mastered the art of reading a map book, a useful tool to which I initially gave little credit. We covered how to approach any type of interview—whether the parties were angry and animated or just calm—with the appropriate distance, gun "bladed" away from the interview. Officer Howe instructed me on details I had never read in a text-book, such as how, when conducting an interview, you shouldn't hold your pad and pen up high by your chest and shoulders, but near your waist, so that you're that much closer to your gun and radio if things go to shit. Being taught things I had never seen in a textbook became a predominant theme my entire rookie year.

Once I finally got used to Officer Howe and how he did things, I was switched to my second field training officer, Dave Adams. All I knew about Dave was that he loved smoking Camel cigarettes, worked second shift, and was predominantly on the north side of town. What I came to learn about Dave was that he was an excellent police officer with a real knack for street smarts and was certifiably crazy behind the wheel of a patrol cruiser. Although I had done a fair amount of driving with Officer Howe, Dave just looked at me and said, "Ah, no." He drove the whole four weeks and spent an equal amount of time on the road, running through people's yards in several chases and responding to emergencies. I learned a great deal from Dave in those weeks, mainly on the importance of keeping my mouth shut around other more experienced officers until I was at least through with my probationary year. This would become a lesson I saw many newer officers fail over the years and sadly saw them struggle to find their place within the department. Simply put, the paramilitary world of police work demands that respect is earned, and starting off as a loudmouth rookie will not accomplish this.

I wrapped up my training with Officer Carter Bright, another experienced officer who unfortunately had just lost his sister to a tragic illness. Over the years I came to admire Carter as a smart cop with really good instincts, and he taught me a lot, especially during the later supervisory years. But the days we spent in FTO were mainly in silence, and I respected the difficult time he was going through. After our four weeks, it was back to Officer Howe for final evaluation, and then I was sent out on my own. Though technically still a cub for the first year, you definitely didn't get called one every day once you were out on your own. The trade-off, however, was that you were on your own with all the responsibility that came with it.

5

IDEALISM

As I mentioned earlier, no police officers forget their first day on the job. But for me it's the first year that I can't forget. During all of my interviews for police officer, I'd been asked why I wanted to be one. I then launched into a long answer about how I wanted to help people when they most need it and to make the community a better place for all the citizens to live in. The truth is that while most police officers genuinely want to help people, they are drawn to the danger and excitement of the job. There are many other professions in which you could safely help your community and the people in it without exposing yourself to injury or even death. But that's the key to understanding younger police officers: they all see themselves as invincible and incapable of being seriously hurt on the job. They go to work with a false sense of security and carry that into their everyday assignments.

A veteran officer told me something years later that highlighted this point best about newer, idealistic police officers: "Year one, they are dangerous because they have no idea what they're doing. But year five they are the most dangerous they will ever be on the job, because they believe they are still invincible combined with the attitude of believing they know everything about the job." A truer statement was never made in police work. Understanding it, though, is a lot more complex.

All officers start out with the idealistic nature that drove them to become police in the first place. They genuinely want to help people and make their lives better. Most of them want to work hard and get involved in what is called *proactive policing*: not just responding to calls for service but actively looking for crime and policing it in their assigned neighborhood. Proactive policing can range from something as simple as writing a ticket to surveillance in a high-drug or high-crime area and stopping people who look reasonably suspicious. Newer officers should want to do these things or they're in for a long slog of a career.

I started out with every belief that I was able to change the world, or at least Battle Creek, through policing. I attacked each day by responding to as many calls as I could, along with making traffic stops and writing tickets. The more proactive policing I engaged in, the more arrests I made. This led to car and foot chases and to fights when suspects resisted arrest. The more excitement I could get, the better. The first months I was a cop were psychologically the easiest ones of my career, mainly because I didn't yet know what was going to start tearing me down. These were truly the best years I experienced because most calls were newer and full of discovery of and exposure to a darker side of life I'd never seen in my sheltered upbringing. Not only did I think I could make a difference, I believed I already had each and every day. For example, when I locked up a cocaine user or dealer, I believed I had made Battle Creek a better place. On the surface I obviously had, or so it seemed.

Around my second year on the job I started noticing some things. Whenever I arrested drug users or street-level dealers, there were always others to replace them. Drugs were not going away, whether Nancy Reagan told us to "just say no" or not. But it wasn't just drugs that I started seeing differently. Calls for service at repeated addresses did not change the behavior of the people we were trying to help. We saw repeated cases of domestic abuse, substance use, and all the crimes that go along with them. There was a never-ending cycle of violence with loosely affiliated gangs all over the city. Serious alcohol-related car accidents kept happening no matter how many drunk drivers we arrested. Over and over it became apparent that the things we did every day as officers were going to be done again tomorrow and the next day and the next. The reality that what we did was going to be done repeatedly for the same types of incidents, call after call, began to chip away at that initial halo of idealism we came to the job with. Each chip built on the next one until we began to face whether we were making a difference.

It's important to realize that all cops come to this reality early in their careers. It's part of the metamorphosis from cubbie to officer to veteran officer. This progression isn't a bad thing in creating effective officers. Too idealistic, and you'll find yourself unprepared to handle the daily barrage of crap that is going to be thrown at you. You need to be able to combat the reality facing you daily, and for me that came in the form of some very specific incidents.

During my first year, I was commuting back and forth from Grand Rapids because I hadn't secured housing in Battle Creek. After one of my initial day shifts while I was still in FTO training, I was northbound on M-37 in my personal car and still partially in uniform. Nearing the city limits of Kentwood, I saw a red vehicle a ways off, southbound on M-37 coming toward me. The vehicle was driving recklessly and might have eventually hit me. However, it came to a stop in the middle of the road. As I approached the sports car I noticed the driver was pale, his head back, and his mouth open. The car doors were locked, so using a wrench given to me by the driver of a passing tool truck, I smashed the window and got the driver out. A young lady assisted me, we administered CPR, and we saved the guy's life. He was in his late fifties. What I didn't know was that this man was a doctor in Battle Creek whose specialization in ear, nose, and throat medicine would help my second son's hearing difficulties years later. The experience hit me hard, as I realized that people could die at a much younger age than that of the elderly grandparents I had seen die.

Another call that changed me was in the Post-Addition neighborhood. A girl had been heard crying. The complainant said the girl would not stop crying on and off, day and night, and thought she might be next door. He wasn't sure because the noise was sometimes faint. We walked around a few of the houses in the area and were about to leave having heard nothing until my assisting officer, Dave Adams, heard something that sounded like crying coming from a basement window well. I heard it too once he pointed it out, we knocked on the door repeatedly, and we received no answer.

We eventually made an emergency forced entrance into the house and found a couple of men in the kitchen who tried to run out the back when we entered. Once we detained them, we checked the basement where the crying was coming from and found two young girls under age ten who had been locked in a bedroom. The investigation that followed showed that the men had sexually abused the young girls and had collected money from others who abused them as well. I can't erase the look of the pain on their faces from months of abuse and mistreatment.

These children had been victimized by monsters. I had never seen this level of evil in my sheltered life in Grand Rapids, and it took a big chunk of my idealism away all at once.

A call that also stands out in my first couple of years was one in which a woman in her thirties had been held in a closet by her abusive boyfriend and repeatedly tortured. He was merciless to her, inflicting cigarette burns and beating her with an electrical cord. He had even dislocated her arm. I had assisted several officers in finding the woman and arresting her abuser. But what I was so amazed at and not prepared for is how angry she was with all of us for what we had done. She cursed all of us for arresting her boyfriend and was so angry that we had to physically restrain her as she spit on us and tried to pummel us. I was shocked by how much disdain she had for the police. I wondered to myself, "What are we doing here?"

Things were starting to make less sense to me the more calls I went on. Wasn't it supposed to be the opposite? Weren't we supposed to know more the longer we were on the job? This is certainly true, but during the breakdown of idealism in any cop come confusion, experience, and the very start of a backpack, that place into which you can stuff your problems and trauma and simply not deal with them.

Being a rookie cop was not all work though. In every police department, no matter how big or small, there is an unwritten hazing of each new group of rookies as they venture out into the job. This process is more important than it may appear. Every new cop comes into the job green and wet behind the ears, but the character trait they all have in abundance is trust. You won't find this in any of your police academy textbooks, but trust in your fellow humans is probably the worst thing you can have on the job. A cynical cop is an effective cop. Trusting the public can get you injured or killed. Human nature makes us want to trust our fellow humans. We want to see the good in others. To work the streets, though, you can't make a habit of trusting what you see on the job. The only trust you want to develop is in the brother or sister in blue standing by your side. That's why the timeless tradition of rookie hazing is so important. It builds the bond between cops, while at the same time teaching an important lesson about trust.

There is no specific way that a rookie is tested by veterans. I have seen everything from a locker filled with shaving cream because the rookie left it unlocked to a snake being left in a patrol car. Most of the pranks involve a rookie simply being too trusting and green. Other pranks take place because the rookie is a loudmouth and needs to be knocked down a few pegs. Either way, all rookies are tested and will be better for it when they grow in experience and maturity. My best example of rookie hazing came toward the end of my first year and was memorable enough that the story is still retold around BCPD today.

I had joined a team of ten officers that was also an off-duty pistol shooting team. We had practiced for several weeks to compete in Jackson, Michigan, at a state pistol competition against over a hundred officers. I was excited to be part of a veteran group and felt I had turned the corner on being a rookie. I can only laugh and smile looking back now.

We arrived in Jackson as a group and after checking into our hotel headed to dinner. Having matched my teammates beer for beer, I was feeling pretty good and having a great time. We arrived at a local steak house and ordered steaks all around. And then the waitress arrived with a tray full of double shots of vodka. One of the senior guys yelled, "It's time to take this party up a notch!" and proceeded to down his shots. He then put his arm around me and said, "You're hangin' with the big dogs now, rook'; think you can hang?" I just gave him a goofy smile and slammed my drink. Ten minutes later another tray of double shots arrived, and then another. By the time dinner arrived, we had consumed over eight shots of vodka, mainly on an empty stomach. Or so I thought. Unbeknownst to me, one of the guys had paid the waitress to deliver a tray of water in glasses each round to everyone except me. As dinner arrived they were all basically stone sober while I was more drunk than a fraternity brother on spring break.

Dinner started with my vague recollection of eating my steak with my hands, like a caveman. I recall attacking my food and a lot of laughter at the table. Having no idea that I was the only intoxicated guy, I must have thought we were all as drunk as I was. It had to be quite a sight. The next thing I knew we all piled into Art McClenny's van and drove through downtown Jackson looking for a bar. As we cruised the streets, somewhere in the blur something caught my eye and I yelled for Art to stop the van. Most of the guys just started laughing, until one of them said, "What the hell. Let's see what he does." What I had seen was a sign for a karaoke contest inside the bar. I was too drunk to realize that the parking lot was filled only with Harley-Davidson motorcycles.

When I entered the bar, I noticed how full it was and that everyone looked like a biker. I remember as we first walked in hearing one of our guys say, "Man, I don't know about this. Maybe we should get out of here." I didn't give them a chance. What I did next I doubt I'll ever do again in my life. It defied all logic, sense, and reason. Without telling anyone in my group what I was doing, I walked straight through the center of the crowded room toward the stage, where a rather large biker all in leather was singing some song. I stepped onto the stage while he was singing and grabbed the mic right out of his hand. How I didn't get punched right there I'll never know. I think he and everyone else were just curious what this skinny twenty-one-year-old was going to do. I didn't disappoint.

With slurred speech, I started by apologizing to the guy I had just grabbed the mic from and told the crowd, "I've got something special for y'all tonight!" The person presumably in charge tried to take the mic back from me, but the guy to whom I'd just apologized smiled and said, "No, let him go. I wanna hear this!" The floor was now all mine. As I looked out at a room full of leather and long beards, I told everyone that I would be "touching their very souls this evening as I went back to their childhood." Then I began to sing: "Here's the story of a lovely lady…" I could see that despite my drunk and likely off-key singing, the crowd liked my song. They began to clap as I sang the second verse, and when I got to the chorus I told everyone to "sing with me." Remarkably all those bikers did just that as we all sang, "The Brady Bunch, the Brady Bunch, that's the way we became the Brady Bunch!" Everyone gave me a standing ovation as the song ended, and I jumped off the stage and high-fived my way through the crowd. We left the bar just as fast as we had arrived. To this day I have no idea if I won the singing contest, but it sure was fun.

Back at the hotel room, I ended the night in the bathroom regretting all of the vodka I had so willingly consumed. The next morning I was regretting it even more. When we arrived at the pistol shoot, I was not in good physical condition. I couldn't drink enough water. I probably shouldn't have been participating in the contest, and that became clear when it was my turn to shoot. I was a decent shot, but in my hungover state my wrist didn't feel steady. After my series of shots, the targets were brought forward and suddenly the guy next to me started cursing up a storm. He was furious and said he was a two-time champion and would never shoot that far outside his target. A bullet hole was on the edge of his target outside the scoring range. I knew it had to be from me. When they looked at my target, my shots were all over the place. They let the guy reshoot, and I agreed to remove myself from the tournament due to inexperience. Ha! Inexperience was a good word for it. Lesson learned, though, as I realized that trust was something I needed to consider carefully. It was a good bonding experience, though, and from that moment on my nickname from the guys was "Bobby," from Bobby Brady, the television family's youngest son.

6

THE DAILY GRIND

Most people's experiences with a cop are either at some of the worst moments of their lives or when they're involved in a traffic crash or committing a traffic infraction. Bottom line, their experience is generally not a pleasant one. The challenge for any officer is to make these moments in a person's life less stressful, more tolerable, and if possible even pleasant. This is the true mark of what it means to be a professional, and in a profession that is increasingly scrutinized by the public, it makes being a police officer one of the hardest jobs a person can have. Today's officers work their shifts with a body camera and vehicle camera recording their every move. Those split-second decisions that an officer is required to make are later analyzed under the microscope of recorded video and public opinion. Yet over a million brave men and women suit up each day and continue to police our nation's streets. They continue to do one of the most difficult jobs, day in and day out, striving toward the goal of being the best and most professional officers they can be. This book is for them as they clip on the gun belts for the daily grind.

I began my fifth year on the job working in a drug enforcement unit called the Neighborhood Enforcement Team (NET). This was a sought-after unit in which to work at the BCPD, and I was enjoying the change in pace from being a responder to traditional 911 calls to having our designated radio channel and focusing on going after drug users and dealers. One of the things that is important for officers in the development of their careers is to balance their experiences with different types of police work. Some officers choose to work undercover, others decide to join the detective bureau, and many work in supervision and command. It's an exception to see officers work their entire career in patrol as a 911 responder without some injection of variety. Day in and day out 911 calls are a recipe for burnout more so than any other aspect of police work. The strain of repeatedly dealing with people's negativity will often lead to a jaded perspective after years of being beaten down by the same problems. I have seen really good officers who, within ten years of consistent patrol work, burn out to the point that they either quit or begin to make very stupid decisions that they would not have made earlier in their careers.

My decision to join the Neighborhood Enforcement Team came at just the right time in my career. I was not on the job long enough in five years to burn out, but I could see where I might be led one day. It's hard to explain what I mean by this, but any officer who handles ten to fifteen or even more 911 calls a day can tell you what that does to you over a period of years. I guess the best way to put it is that you sort of go on autopilot and become callous toward others' problems and concerns, which is not a good mix for a cop to have. So, as I started working the

NET, I was excited to make a difference once again. At least that was the goal.

Six of us worked in the Neighborhood Enforcement Team. The seventh member was our sergeant, Mark Pierce. Sergeant Pierce was a by-the-book guy who had a very regimented approach to police work. If you had a suspended license, you went to jail. If you had any amount of marijuana on you, you went to jail. He was also a great supervisor to work for, as he was one of those sergeants who would always have your back. If you needed him on one of your traffic stops, he would be there in minutes or less. You didn't always agree with him, but he'd hear you out. As far as they went, you didn't work for too many supervisors on the street as good as he was.

Our primary assignment was to deal with whatever the road patrol divisions couldn't, which could be any type of crime or issue within the city. If there was a major drug area that was creating a spike in crimes such as shootings, larcenies, or break-ins, then we would work that area and target those homes in which people were selling drugs. If there was an area flooded with complaints of prostitutes, then we'd work that problem. If there was a parade that needed to be worked, we often were reassigned to traffic control for that event. It was essentially the problem-solving unit for the city and was generally never boring or monotonous.

We worked the unit using our own radio channel and therefore gave each other radio code names in case our channel was ever hacked, but mainly because we could, and so we did. My radio handle was "Tinker," derived from my last name. Sergeant Pierce was "Kato," Calvin Newlands was "Noodles," Mike Bradley was "Dolomite," Esteban Rivera was "Chumley," Grady Pierce was "Gadget," and my favorite was Wayne Smith's "Big

Fruity." Overall it was a great team of to be a part of, and it developed into a close-knit group as we had only each other to rely on most of the time. We could always call the 911 units to assist us, but often they wouldn't know exactly which area we were working.

Just such a situation happened to me on a hot summer afternoon when we were working a major drug area in the Washington Heights district. I was working by myself and most of the team members had gone on their meal break. I had eaten earlier in the shift so I was wandering around our beat when I noticed a guy I recognized as a crack user and corner dealer. He was walking into and out of the street, which wasn't uncommon for people to do in the summer, but something didn't look right. The longer I watched him from about half a block away, I started to realize he was carrying on a conversation with himself to the point that he was motioning with his hands. I moved closer and made my first officer safety mistake.

Let me pause here and highlight something important about how officers get injured on the job. There is usually not one but several seemingly small officer safety mistakes that all add up to the ultimate injury. Unfortunately, many of these injuries are serious and in some cases fatal. Although not every injury in police work is preventable, given the dangerous nature of the job itself, this incident certainly was.

When I got out of the police car, I was alone without backup approaching a known drug user I wasn't getting a good vibe about. Mistake number two was when I got out of the car, I failed to notify any NET teammates on our channel that I was making contact with the suspect. Mistake number three was my failure to notify central dispatch on channel 1 where I was or what I was doing. The mistakes were starting to pile up and I hadn't even spoken to the guy yet.

When I approached him he was still carrying on a conversation with himself and would not answer my direct questions: "Where are you coming from, Cedell?" and "Where are you heading to?" He did provide me with his date of birth, which I used to run his information through the Law Enforcement Information Network (LEIN). This is a national and local network that can give an officer information about whether a person is missing, is wanted for an arrest warrant, has a criminal history, or is in the United States illegally. LEIN allows officers to compile critical information and share it across jurisdictional lines. The LEIN operator gave me information that the guy was wanted for several felony warrants involving cocaine delivery and use.

Writing out the mistakes I made on this one citizen contact is painful and embarrassing to see in words, even years later, but also an excellent example of how an officer with over five years' experience can get into trouble in seconds by forgetting basic training. Mistake number four was my decision to arrest the suspect by myself. Again, I could have waited for a backup unit to arrive, knowing he had a confirmed felony warrant, and I chose not to. I told him to put his hands against the car, which he did, but when I reached for his right wrist to pull his arm behind his back for handcuffing, he spun around and swung his elbow, striking me in the side of the head and nearly knocking me out. Stunned, I stumbled backward while the suspect, instead of fleeing, charged at me, tackled me, and pulled me to the ground. I was on my back, and he started punching me repeatedly in my face and head. My only recourse was to block my face and punch when I could. The suspect had a crazed look on his face, and he was relentless. I managed to turn onto my side and caught him square on the chin, knocking him back enough for me to get up and back on my feet. I was dizzy from being punched and knew, now that I was out of his grasp, that I needed to notify dispatch.

Mistake number five was a compilation of the other mistakes before it. I grabbed my radio, pressed the button, and yelled, "Officer needs assistance. Fight." However, before I could say more the suspect ran at me again, wildly swinging his fists and trying to tackle me. We managed to stay on our feet this time, and both of us were getting tired, but he wasn't quitting. Even though both of us were in our twenties, it was becoming apparent that given his lack of rational thinking and better-than-average strength for a fairly skinny guy, he was also on some type of drug. It had been at least a couple of minutes, a very long time for altercations. I noticed a crowd was starting to gather in the area but not right near us. I yelled for someone to call the dispatchers and tell them our location, but every time I reached for my radio the suspect was still punching. Again, he tackled me, but this time I felt him tugging at my gun. I remember the fear I felt as I realized that if he got my gun or I was somehow knocked unconscious, I would likely be shot and killed. Despite the twist-and-turn safety holster, he pulled on the gun so that it started coming out of the holster. I grabbed his arm with both my hands and pushed the gun back down into the holster. We wrestled like this for a few seconds, during which I managed to kick him in groin. He then staggered back, allowing me to resecure my handgun.

The suspect then decided to run. I gave chase, while telling dispatch where I was, or so I thought. However, I had been on channel 5 (the channel designated to the Neighborhood Enforcement Team) the entire time. The only officers hearing me were the guys in our unit. If you were outside a certain radius on our channel, you couldn't hear much of anything clearly. So my team members caught only bits and pieces. Thankfully, when they heard me yelling, they told the central dispatchers the area we were working in so they could send patrol units that were closer to my location.

I continued chasing the suspect, who started hopping fences and running through backyards. I only knew vaguely what street we were on. Then, in one of the yards, confirming that he had to be on some kind of drug, the suspect turned and ran at me, tackled me again, and threw me to the ground. Both of us were very tired and slower, but we continued to wrestle. Unfortunately, he wasn't done. I felt him bite the side of my neck as though he were a vampire. The bite broke the skin but could have been much worse than it actually was. Patrol units all over the area were looking for us, and when one of the neighbors flagged Officer Cooper down, we finally got the suspect handcuffed and arrested.

I look back on this incident firmly smacking my forehead while shaking my head at how fortunate I was to come out on top and alive. But the lessons I have been able to pass on to students in the Police Academy have been some of the most important I could ever teach them. First, I was in the best physical condition of my life at this point. My coworker Cal Newlands and I ran and lifted weights almost every day. Nothing can prepare you better for the job than staying in shape. This fight with the suspect took over ten minutes, and if I had been in poor shape I could have been killed. Second, the series of mistakes I made were all preventable. Safety is rarely something that officers look back on and say they did all they could. Officers get ambushed, and often the job is simply dangerous. Had I taken the precautionary measures I was trained to use, the arrest would have been much more routine and controlled. This is what happens to some officers around their fifth year on the job: an overconfidence in their own abilities. Nobody taught me that this type of attitude was something to guard against, and I wish someone had.

Entering the second half of the 1990s, I continued working with the Neighborhood Enforcement Team. But working on the team was only a two-year assignment and I returned to road patrol, responding to 911 calls. The daily grind continued as one domestic violence call led to another, and one car accident led to two more.

There were routines, of course, like getting coffee and meeting up with other officers to catch up on what was going on in our lives. As I look back, the one thing I miss the most about being a cop is the strong bond you have with other officers. They are the ones you spend the most time with and who understand you as nobody else can. You meet—or "clatch up"—car to car to swap stories from the shift and vent about internal politics that exist in every police department. After years of having hundreds of these discussions, officers cement the bond between them for a lifetime.

But there is a serious consequence. As officers vent to each other about the job and the trauma they all deal with, they come to rely on only each other. They subconsciously close ranks and over time come to believe that only someone with a badge can even remotely comprehend them and realize what they're going through. This is certainly true to a degree, but the subtle danger is that the people officers love the most in their lives usually get left behind.

7

SO YOU WANT
TO BE A COP?

Over the course of my career hundreds of people have asked me, "Why did you want to become a cop?" or "What's it like to be a cop?" People are genuinely interested in the job, as evidenced by the limitless television shows and movies surrounding the profession. From Sheriff Andy in Mayberry to *Hill Street Blues* and *NYPD Blue*, the shows just keep coming, some more realistic than others. Although a few have come fairly close, no show or movie can adequately represent what it's like to put on the uniform and actually "be a cop."

As I've detailed, I did not become a cop the conventional way and really never wanted or intended to be one. And looking at any graduating police academy class today, you'll find there are more diverse and unique backgrounds leading to the badge. This has been the biggest change to a profession that was throughout most of the last century a predominantly white male one. The complexities of why this has changed are the subject of books and many theses and dissertations. Whether you're white, black, brown, Christian, Muslim, Jewish, male or female, none of it matters when you put on the uniform. You'll hear a cop say, "I bleed blue." This a more powerful statement than it may at first seem. It means, "I am part of something bigger than myself, in which my race, background, and personal life take a backseat to the mission to which I commit myself each day: protecting my fellow officers and the community I serve. This doesn't mean you don't still have personal beliefs and a unique personality. It means you don't get to always put those things first on the job.

So you want to be a cop? Well, this is the first thing you have to be able to accept: that you will bleed blue. And bleeding blue is not always what many people can deal with. Let me highlight this point with a personal example. As a Christian, I believe that you must put God first in your life, and his law is what you must follow. Yet as a police officer you will find that your personal beliefs may conflict with your duties on the job. Just such a situation occurred to me early in my career. I was working one of the city's south-side districts, and several officers were tasked with responding to Planned Parenthood, where a large protest was occurring. There was a sit-in, and many people were blocking the entrance to the clinic to protest abortion. This was in clear violation of state and local laws, and as police officers we were tasked with it.

If the five or six officers dispatched to deal with the protesters were responding based on their personal beliefs, then we would have been quite a mix in how we approached the situation. Several of my coworkers are pro-choice, might have become emotionally involved, and dealt angrily with the protesters. Other coworkers are pro-life, might have identified with the protesters, and not tried to move them. Could you imagine the scene? This is the very essence of laws and why we have them. It is why we call our profession "law enforcement." So, on this day my personal beliefs, regardless of what they are, did not dictate how I acted. They likewise did not dictate how my fellow officers acted either. We simply enforced the law respectfully and professionally.

First, we informed the protesters that by blocking access to the clinic on private property they were violating the law. Then we requested they leave the property immediately, no longer block access to the entrance to the clinic, and return their protest legally to public property. Several protesters did get up at that point and move, while three or four chose to stay lying down in front of the door. At that point we placed those who remained under arrest for violating the law of trespassing. So, you want to be a police officer? First, you have to be able to uniformly bleed blue. That's why many people are not able to work as cops.

The second thing I tell people who want to be a cop is that you must have courage and the ability to manage your fear. The veteran officer will always answer the question "Are you afraid working as a cop?" with "Yes. If you're not afraid, you're not being honest." This is absolutely true. From some of the earliest calls I handled to the very end of my career, I was faced with numerous circumstances in which I was genuinely afraid. Now, did I tell my coworkers, "Man, I sure was scared on that call!"? No, that just isn't done. But there was rarely a week I didn't face a scenario in which I felt genuine fear. The rookie will respond to the same question about fear by telling you, "No. I'm not afraid or I couldn't become or be a cop." I felt that way once. It's an answer born of ignorance and lack of experience.

But it's not the fear that will keep you from being a cop. It's the inability to have courage and manage that fear. Failure to have courage will keep you from working as an effective cop, and if you continue to work, you might become a dangerous one. Although not every call an officer goes on is outwardly dangerous, many are. There is no end to the number of examples I could give here, but I'll highlight a few any beat cop would relate to.

When I was in my first year and out on my own, I found myself on night shift working with a group of officers I didn't know very well. I didn't understand many of the unwritten rules of working night shift, such as "Cover your own district's calls before you engage in proactive policing such as making traffic stops" or "Kill your headlights and overheads at least two blocks from your call on a breaking and entering and never hit your brakes when you stop; use the parking brake." Night shift is its own ecosystem and is not policed effectively without experience. But before any of that experience can be gained, officers must first have courage and the ability to manage their fear.

It was shortly after midnight on a busy Friday night when dispatch put out a be-on-the-lookout (BOLO) for a "suspect vehicle, late eighties black Cadillac, involved in a shooting/ homicide in Kalamazoo, unknown registration with damage to left side bumper and taillight, occupants four black males in their late teens, should be considered armed and dangerous." I wrote the details down on my pad and continued the shift. About an hour later a black Cadillac matching the general description blew through a stop sign in front of me. I pulled in behind it, and it started to speed away from me. I noticed as I increased speed and got closer that the vehicle did not have a registration plate but did have a decent-sized amount of damage to the left rear bumper and taillight. I called dispatch requesting backup as I followed the vehicle, waiting to turn the overhead lights on until I knew how close backup was.

To say I was afraid would be to put it extremely mildly. My heart was pounding out of my chest, and I expected to see guns at any moment turned toward me out of the windows and begin firing. With backup behind me I initiated a traffic stop on the suspect vehicle and expected a pursuit to ensue. Instead, to my shock the car simply pulled over. My heart was pounding so hard now that I could barely think straight. And this is where police officers must learn to manage their fear and courageously continue to handle the stressful circumstances before them.

We positioned our vehicles to conduct what is called a *felony stop*, in which officers must use their loudspeaker to give instructions to the driver and any other occupants of the vehicle to maximize officer safety and handle the stop efficiently. The felony stop is reserved for traffic stops on vehicles in which danger is expected. It cannot be used in a hunch. A potential suspect vehicle from a BOLO on a homicide certainly qualified. As I fumbled my way through my first felony stop, first giving instructions to the driver to remove the keys, I could hear my own voice crack. I only hoped my fellow officers didn't notice. Next, I asked the driver to step out of the car, hold his hands above his head, walk backward toward us, stop, and turn 360 degrees so we could view his waistband for any potential weapons.

Then I ordered him to lie flat on the ground with his hands behind him. I repeated these instructions to all the other passengers. Once all were lying flat on the ground, two officers handcuffed the occupants while the other officers covered them by holding their weapons in a safe position but ready to use if needed. At the same time, two other officers checked the vehicle and trunk for any other occupants; you never want to assume there aren't more just because they didn't respond to your commands. There are a lot of moving parts to a proper felony stop, and the night-shift officers I was working with were very good at them and at working together as a team.

The vehicle was connected to the Kalamazoo homicide, but the occupants were only witnesses and later released. The vehicle was held as evidence. Although I was extremely nervous and definitely afraid, I managed that fear and worked my way through the stressful event. A few officers left police work very early in their careers because they couldn't manage this fear. Nothing is wrong with that. After you have gone through the police academy and all that training, to be able to admit that policing is not the job for you takes a tremendous amount of courage. I admired officers who admitted this and got out. They therefore weren't dangers to themselves and their fellow cops.

Officers who are afraid and incapable of managing their fear, yet remain on the job, are the most concerning. All officers can name one or two such officers in their department. They're not hard to pick out, because over time they expose themselves through how they act on stressful calls. They are often in the last car to arrive at a critical scene every time and are rarely seen as leaders. They routinely make dangerous mistakes in officer safety and as a result retreat further into a shell of inadequacy. So, you want to be a police officer? Make sure first that you are someone who can manage your fears. If you find you are unable to do so, then there is no shame in chalking this career up as another life experience and moving on to something else.

The third thing I tell people thinking about becoming cops is that they should not expect to hear "Thank you" or "Good job." If they are looking for those things, I tell them to consider becoming a firefighter, although I suspect they don't get enough praise either. Police officers get fewer thank-yous and less admiration than do customer service representatives working for an airline on a busy holiday weekend. People don't usually love cops. That is becoming a growing attitude despite efforts to bridge those gaps. But lack of thanks isn't something unheard of. As a police officer you'll see people at their most negative and during their worst experiences. The last thing most people will want to say is "Thank you," and when they do, it won't usually sound heartfelt.

Over time this wears down a cop's idealism and chips away like water on a stone. Eventually, the stone develops a crack. Cops are human after all. So, you want to be a cop? Have a thick skin or get some.

During a call early in my career, two parents in their late twenties were distraught about their nine-year-old daughter, who had not returned home from school as usual. This was a serious call, and not only did the road patrol become involved but detectives from the bureau were also called in. The girl had not taken the bus but had been in school all day. Classmates and teachers recalled seeing her, and nothing seemed out of the ordinary until she hadn't returned home on the bus. Nearly three hours since the close of school a lot of anxiety built up when she wasn't found. Every cop knew the evil that lives in every community unseen. Most people are never exposed to this evil, but cops are and know its potential. I was just hoping and praying this girl was not mixed up in something horrible.

Then one of the older, veteran detectives arrived—Al Tolf, aka "Minnow." I have no idea how he got his nickname, but I always thought of him as being like a minnow, always on the scene quickly and right in the middle of things. Al Tolf was one of the greatest detectives you'll hear about, and every department has a few like him. He was a seasoned veteran, with quick reactions but a slow and methodical approach that allowed him to be a sponge for information. Minnow would calmly listen to you, occasionally asking questions but letting you talk, so that he learned more and more. I often joked with him that I would try not to talk with him too long myself, because I wasn't sure what I might confess.

On this day, Minnow had spent a good fifteen or twenty minutes talking to the distressed parents. I watched him as he listened to them very carefully, letting them vent to him and talk nonstop. He occasionally wrote a note on his pad but generally just listened intently and nodded his head from time to time. After he was done, he said, "C'mon kid, let's go see if we can't find this girl." I joined him in his detective car, and we started driving toward the Battle Creek River. As a newer cop I was still talking too much. I asked Minnow, "You don't think she drowned, do you? What do you think happened? Where are we going?" I probably sounded like one of my kids on a long car ride.

Minnow listened to me for a while. Then he lit a cigarette and said, "Assume nothing, but listen to everything they tell you." I said something to him like "Is that how you handle a missing person call?" But I'll never forget his answer: "No, kid, it's how you handle every call." I never forgot that and told this story to many younger cops over the years.

We arrived at the river and slowly drove along Riverside Drive on the banks. Minnow just told me to look for a girl in a reddish-blue coat and pink rubber boots. After about twenty minutes Minnow calmly lit another cigarette and looked at me. "You wanna get her, kid?" He pointed toward one of the banks near a street called Burnham Drive, where she was sitting and playing with a boatlike toy on a string, seemingly without a care in the world. We drove closer. I got out of the car, walked up to her, and asked if her parents knew where she was. She was enjoying playing and told me that she was Pocahontas, the character from the 1995 Disney movie of the same name who was seen canoeing on the river and was in general often around water.

Minnow told me later that this is why he believed she might be near the river: she lived in this neighborhood, and her parents had told him that she was lately obsessed with Pocahontas. I was stunned that this small detail had been so crucial and had led to her recovery. Although a neighbor or family friend could have located her or she could have walked home on her own eventually, I did find out later that she could not swim and therefore may have been in more danger. Minnow was one of the greats and is deservedly still talked about today.

But that's not the end of this story. When we got back to the house with the girl, it was so rewarding to see her run from my car and into the desperate and anxious arms of her parents. I walked up to them to summarize the details of what she was doing when the father cut me off stating, "If you had been doing your jobs, this shit wouldn't happen." He berated me about how police officers should be present at the close of school and simply not let children walk away alone and unattended. Apparently, the young girl had missed her bus and just walked home, stopping to play near the river. The father was very upset that the police hadn't noticed and thus endangered his daughter and nearly got her killed. Obviously, there were several flaws in his logic, but as an officer this was not the time to have this conversation with this dad. Minnow simply tapped my shoulder and nodded his head for us to leave.

Not once did either parent thank us. Twenty or more police and school officials aided in the search for several hours. Every resource we had was being used, from dog tracking to mobilization of the civilian emergency response team.

I was really pissed off, and Minnow noticed. As we got out of the car later he said, "Look, kid, if you're looking for an 'attaboy' or some kind of award and thanks for this job, then I gotta bridge to sell ya." He chuckled, lit up another smoke, and walked away. Another lesson learned by someone with thirty years on the job.

Police work is not a job for the thin-skinned, the faint of heart, the stubborn, or those unable to compromise. It is not a job for those without the courage to step into the fray. Taxpayers are not going to care unless you screw up. The job is not for those seeking affirmation at every turn and medals for the mundane.

Police officers' jobs are to step every day into the shoes of those who can't fill them, to do so with the anonymity of ghosts, and to simply be guardians and protectors in blue of each person they serve.

So, you want to be a cop? I couldn't be prouder of you. Just know that what lies ahead is bigger than each of you, and yet together as one big blue family you can care for, handle, and take one call at a time. And those who served before you, the Heffs and the Minnows, will guide you through the generations to protect the communities and streets they gave so much to. To all of you past, present, and yet to come, I say, "Thank you! Job well done!"

8

"DO YOU REMEMBER WHEN?" OR EVERYONE HAS A STORY

Get any group of cops together and you'll find no end to the stories they will tell of things they've seen and done in their careers. It doesn't matter if some are newer officers or retired. There's just a bottomless supply of material to lead from one story to another, often with some thread from the previous story to move the conversation along. Every profession has its water cooler or faculty lounge chatter, but it's the type of stories that officers have that separate them from any other profession. The stories are one of a kind and often do not need embellishment to capture your attention. Some are funny, some sad, others tragic and serious. The cathartic rhythm of a group of cops telling stories is yet another unique and special reason to become one. One of them shouts, "Do you remember when?" and the stories begin.

I was working a busy afternoon shift, with one car accident leading to another and one domestic argument leading to another. All the officers were just as busy and the dispatcher was talking nearly nonstop trying to keep up. It was a very hot summer day, with little wind or relief from the heat. It wasn't uncommon to actually sweat off a few pounds on days like these because of the bulletproof vest under the polyester uniform. The hotter the weather, the more the calls and the busier your shift.

What happened next was the last thing any of us had time for. A farmer was hauling a livestock trailer down Emmett Street in the middle of the city. The trailer was wooden, older, and in disrepair. When he lurched to a stop approaching the North Avenue intersection, the rear of the trailer shattered and out came a huge cow. The cow didn't waste an instant of her newfound freedom and started running right down the middle of Emmett Street toward Fremont School, which thankfully was not in session. The farmer was older and didn't know what to do. I didn't have a clue what to do either.

More by instinct and blind stupidity I ran toward the running cow and used my police radio to let others know that I needed a few officers to assist me. The closer I got to the cow, the more I spooked her, and she simply ran away from me. The cow turned onto Fremont Street, and with the help of a few equally frustrated officers, I managed to corral her in a playground at the school. We had a standoff: Battle Creek Police versus huge cow! The cow kept trying to escape from the playground, and we corralled her back into the corner by the merry-go-round. However, none of us knew what to do other than shoot and kill the cow, which we didn't want to do either.

Enter my only real attempt in life to be a cowboy. We acquired a few longer ropes, and I came up with the bright idea that we could fashion a lasso and, like a cowboy, simply control and capture the cow. Easy, right? How hard could it be? After all, we'd seen enough movies! Well, almost an hour later, lots of failed throws, and the cow's quick runs, we were no nearer to getting a lasso around her neck. The cow was breathing heavily and frothing at the mouth, clearly distressed by our attempted madness. I had attempted to contact the Department of Natural Resources (DNR) and animal control officers to tranquilize the animal, but we couldn't get a tranquilizer there for several hours. The shift's calls were piling up and supervisors were increasingly pressuring us to get the hell out of this call.

Then, as though John Wayne and Clint Eastwood had walked into our lives, a couple of cowboys arrived on the scene and in a few short minutes had several well-placed lassos over the cow's neck. They calmly walked the cow to the trailer they had brought, and with a firm handshake our agricultural urban nightmare was over. My son Zachary is almost through college and going to be a career farmer. Through him I have learned the hard work and determination it takes to become a farmer, how special farmers are, and how important they are to the very fiber that makes up our great nation. If you see farmers, thank them for all they do. They don't make a lot of money, and without them we couldn't be who we are. So, to all you farmers out there, "Thank you!"

Do you remember that time when . . . we were working with the Neighborhood Enforcement Team, and Sergeant Tom Reed was working overtime as our supervisor? We were in unmarked cars watching through binoculars from a couple of blocks away as a group of suspected drug dealers played cards and gambled in the front yard of a house that we suspected was also being used to store and deal drugs from. Between four and six people were crammed around the table playing cards on a nice summer afternoon. While the card came was going on, cars pulled up, and we suspected the occupants would purchase drugs and leave as the game continued. We watched for about a half hour and devised a plan.

We decided that we would simply take all our cars—there were three of us—and drive right up to them, grabbing onto whom we could and checking them for drugs, weapons, or open arrest warrants. We decided at the least it would shut the game down and likely somebody would have drugs. As we slowly drove toward the house the table was full of gamblers oblivious to our approach. I was in the lead, with Sergeant Reed behind me and Cal Newlands behind him. As I got within a block I picked up my speed so I could arrive quickly and get out, anticipating that at least one of them would see us soon. When I got within about a house from the suspects, a basketball skipped into the road in front of me, followed by a young boy chasing it. I slammed on my brakes to avoid hitting the boy. Thankfully, I missed him, but my sudden braking caused a chain reaction of events behind me.

To avoid hitting my car, Sergeant Reed swerved sharply to the left and up over the curb, hurtling him straight toward the suspects' playing cards. I was stopped with a front-row seat, as I observed all the card players diving away from the table with incredible speed and dexterity. Because of the speed of our approach and the split-second reaction to swerve left, Sergeant Reed had little if any time to brake. He barreled right into the card table, blasting everything into the air in a plume of cards, money, and shattered table parts. Thankfully, nobody was hurt, and everyone had gotten out of the way in time. Once the young boy got out of the road, Cal and I continued down the street and a few blocks away quickly caught up with Sergeant Reed, who had simply regained control in the roadway and left the area. We found an area behind an abandoned building where we couldn't stop laughing at our unintentional accident. Collectively, we agreed that returning to the scene was not an option, and that the drug dealers were going to get a pass that day for having their card games and possibly their underwear destroyed. Years later, Sergeant Tom and his wife were tragically killed in a car accident together while down south on vacation. They are dearly missed, and his stories are still told today.

Do you remember when ... officers chased a huge black bear in the middle of the city all night long? Another crazy story of which I was not directly a part but so unusual that I had to retell it. Battle Creek is mainly urban, and houses are close together, mainly a product of the blue-collar cereal workers from Post, Kellogg's, and Ralston's, which made our city famous. The Battle Creek River runs through the city. Somehow, on a cool night on the edge of the approaching fall season, a large black bear was seen running through the neighborhoods right near the busy downtown area just after two or three o'clock. This was a full-grown bear, running fast and difficult to keep up with. Officers reported seeing the bear running from roof to roof on houses and garages and sometimes onto trees. They followed the bear for several hours but did not have a tranquilizer available capable of bringing the bear down. The DNR had one but was several hours away in northern Michigan; its animal control employees were heading toward Battle Creek.

The bear appeared scared and was getting increasingly irrational as it sped through, into, and over yards, trees, and roofs. Police officers monitored the bear's location for several hours, which was okay because the city was essentially quiet from three to five o'clock in the morning. But as morning started creeping toward six o'clock, a problem occurred. The supervisor in charge of that area, Sergeant John Chrenenko, later told me the level of stress he felt building as he and other supervisors debated their options. It was a Monday morning, and school was in session.

Soon, schoolkids and their parents would be leaving their houses to head to bus stops. This bear was big, irrational, and potentially dangerous. At the same time none of these officers wanted to kill a bear. John later told me it was truly an incredible animal to see as it moved swiftly along.

Again, another one of those situations that police are put into that requires them to make a decision that, no matter what, will have a litany of armchair quarterbacking to follow. As John later told me: "We had the bear trapped up in a tree at about 6 a.m., and the first light of day was starting to creep into the sky. The DNR said they were still just under an hour away. If we risked leaving the bear in the tree, and it escaped and killed anyone, we would be solely responsible. If we killed the bear now, we would be criticized for animal abuse of some kind. But to me the decision we made was an easy one." Sergeant Chrenenko ordered officers to kill the bear while it was up in the tree, which is what they did. For days many angry citizens second-guessed his decision and the officers' actions. I know without a shadow of a doubt that John made the right call that morning. You always err on the side of public safety and protection. Another one of those reasons being a cop isn't always easy but is never boring.

Do you remember when . . . we worked the night the world was supposed to end? We celebrated the turn of the century on January 1, 2000, not sure if the world was going to come to a crashing halt. Everyone was calling it Y2K, and because of some computer snafu that I still don't fully understand, at the stroke of midnight in each time zone, computers were predicted to crash and consequently lead to mass chaos the world over. Specifically, everything from the electrical grid and security systems to even nuclear power plants was theorized to be vulnerable to breaking down due to the Y2K glitch. Because of the predicted crisis, police officers around the world were ordered into work to deal with the unknown. Command centers were set up in every department to face the calamity that was sure to come. Emergency services commanders had spent months preparing for this night.

As midnight approached, every uniformed officer in the police department was ordered to report for duty. We were assigned a general area to work, but the first thing I remember about this night was how quiet it was. A normal New Year's Eve is usually hopping for the police, bringing call after call to respond to. Perhaps in anxious anticipation of the unknown, it was eerily quiet. The next thing I remember was that although it had not yet reached midnight and the infamous Y2K in America, several places in the world, such as the Middle East and Europe, had already crossed over into the New Year. In none of these places had a single problem occurred involving computer systems, power grids, oil refineries, nuclear power plants, military bases, emergency services, and any other critical area. As hour after hour passed, time zone after time zone crossed into the next century without a peep.

As we neared midnight and the new year, I was assigned to the north side of town. I recall finding a *low spot*, a spot in which you are low enough to avoid any flying bullets, with fellow night shifters Dittmer, Holso, Penning, and Madsen. As any nightshift officer who has policed any New Year's celebrations can tell you, when the ball drops on the new year many people start firing every gun they own into the air. These bullets have to go somewhere so finding a low spot was just for safety until the next call for service came out. Despite the rest of the world not showing any signs of trouble, I was pretty anxious as midnight approached.

As the New Year's Ball dropped in New York City, the usual barrage of gunfire erupted in the city of Battle Creek. It went on for the traditional fifteen minutes or so, as we hunkered down in our patrol cars about twenty feet below ground level in a valley in one of the parks. Bullets occasionally hit trees and branches above us as we chatted and waited for the world to end. After about thirty minutes, though, it became apparent from the relatively quiet police radio that the world as we knew it was still standing. I was one of the sergeants on duty, so I worked my way back to the police station and stopped into our Y2K command center. The chief and all the commanders were working, and seven or eight flat-screen televisions were tuned into different parts of the world. Every one of them was reporting the same thing: no problems.

The great scare known as Y2K was just that, a scare and nothing more. People had stockpiled thousands of canned goods, gallons of water, batteries, emergency band radios, and so many other survival goods, all in anticipation of the potential end of civilization as we know it. But that end never came. The beginning of the end never even came. It was simply one of the most peaceful nights I've ever worked alongside a hundred other officers doing nothing.

9

THE FACE OF EVIL

Evil has a face. Growing up in my sheltered midwestern cocoon of relative safety, I didn't know about the real evil in this world. I read or heard only an occasional newspaper or radio story about some murder or rape that had occurred. Like most people around me, I moved on with a passing comment such as "That's terrible" or "Thank God they caught the guy." But to truly see the face of evil is something most people can't begin to comprehend. Thank God for that. Once you look it in the eyes and see it up close, even worse once you feel it, you know that you'll never be the same again. You'll never trust people the same way, and your view of the world sheds the rosy hope that there is good in everyone. I used to believe that. I want to believe that. But I have seen an evil in some that is so dark that it transcends optimism about every person being capable of change and becoming good. Police officers stand between most people and this face of evil. Police officers never forget those faces, and their nightmares are at times filled with those eyes looking back at them.

My first look into the face of evil came early in my career, shortly after I had shed my rookie label. Detectives were working a homicide in which a sixteen-year-old juvenile had killed a five-year-old girl and dumped her body in a shallow grave in the backyard of an abandoned house where he had killed her. I was at the police station working a regular shift and one of the detectives walked past me with a juvenile boy in handcuffs. We looked at each other, only for a few seconds, and I was stopped in my tracks. His eyes were the coldest, deadest-looking eyes I had ever seen. It chilled me to look at him. I knew nothing at this point about what the boy had done. I didn't even know he was involved in the homicide. But I had never in my short life looked into eyes like that. It was truly like looking into the face of evil.

The details of what this juvenile had done were shocking and certainly confirmed my encounter with him and what I had felt and seen by looking at him. I watched part of the detective's interview with him in the video room and again felt the chilling darkness as he confessed to his brutal crime in a monotone, almost casual manner. He recalled to detectives in graphic detail how on an afternoon in spring he had given the five-year-old two dimes and asked her to get some candy from the store for them to share. He then lured her into the basement of an abandoned house and repeatedly raped and beat her before bludgeoning her to death with a hatchet. He treated her like a piece of trash and not the innocent little girl full of hope that she once was. He stuffed her body into a plastic bag and buried her in a shallow grave in the backyard of the house. I still remember seeing hardened, veteran detectives with tears streaming down their faces as her body was dug up. Throughout the whole ordeal, including the trial, I never once saw the juvenile suspect show one ounce of emotion.

In law enforcement and in life, we often say somebody was evil or committed a terrible crime that made the newspaper that week or month. To commit a murder takes some level of evil inside a person. Hundreds of very bad people deserve to spend the rest of their lives in prison for doing just that. But the dark and depraved level of evil I am referring to is something beyond this. Those people could just as easily stab and kill you as sit down and eat their breakfast and sip their morning coffee, the expression on their faces the same.

About a year later, I once again saw the bone-chilling face of evil. I was still less than five years on patrol as an officer, and I got called to the police station to meet with the supervisor of the Detective Bureau, Commander Newman. He held a briefing highlighting lead Detective Dennis Mullen, who was investigating a Battle Creek homicide and trying to determine if his suspect was involved in any other murders. The suspect was a skinny guy in his late thirties or early forties, who had already confessed to a murder in Arkansas for which he was serving a life sentence. He had abducted a teenaged girl as she was heading to school, and then when he was through he tossed her lifeless body into the woods like a piece of garbage. Years later and already in prison in Arkansas, the suspect confessed to murdering another teenaged girl in Battle Creek. The case became a very controversial one, as the issue of whether the suspect's confession to the Battle Creek murder was actually valid. To this day Detective Mullen believes the Arkansas suspect committed the Battle Creek murder; however the case remains cold and unsolved.

I arrived at the briefing room at the Battle Creek Police Department and listened carefully as Commander Newman detailed the afternoon for us. Officer Dan Smith, several detectives, the murderer from Arkansas, and I all would board a minibus and head to a couple of locations to which the suspect directed us. We wanted to confirm information that only the detectives knew, which would corroborate the suspect's involvement in the murder. The suspect was dressed in an orange jail outfit and secured in standard wraparound belly-chain handcuffs and leg irons. Although we were fairly certain handcuffs and leg irons would be enough to ensure that he did not escape, Officer Smith and I would stand at opposite points ten to fifteen feet apart from him. We were armed with shotguns should anything go wrong. We boarded the minibus and headed to a wooded area outside town.

I sat a couple of rows behind the suspect, close enough to hear him and study his face. He was eerily calm as he spoke in a monotone to detectives and gave them directions. As he guided us to the murder scene, it occurred to me that I showed more emotion ordering a cup of coffee at the local diner than he did discussing the brutal killing of an innocent girl. The deep lines at the corners of his eyes betrayed a long, troubled life. He appeared tired, beat down physically. If I had met this man in a gas station, I would have surmised he needed to get several good nights of sleep. But had I met this man in a gas station, would I be able to tell he was a cold-blooded killer? Normally, I would say no, and this is still the truth. However, any experienced cop who has seen the face of true evil will tell you that the eyes of a killer have a certain look: dark, hollow, empty, soulless. It is a look that masks horrors even our worst nightmares cannot imagine.

As we drove to one of the sites at which a rape and murder were committed, I watched as he directed officers through his hellish past. At some point we were just driving, and the murderer looked over his shoulder at the rest of us in the minibus. For a few seconds we just looked at each other. Chilling. Even terrifying. He looked right through me. I knew at that moment those eyes had seen horrible things. Those eyes displayed the face of evil. I had to look away first, something I don't normally do. It felt as if to look into his eyes longer would hypnotize you. The rest of the day we visited numerous sites and further deepened the mystery of those Battle Creek murders. Was an innocent man already in jail for the murders that this man committed? He's never been prosecuted for them. But I left that day knowing only one thing: whether he killed one or more people in his life, he was certainly capable of killing many. That's what pure evil is.

Over the years, people have asked me what it was like during the trial of my own shooting to come face-to-face with a cold-blooded killer. I remember the trial vividly, and it was certainly an emotional experience so soon after my injury and recovery. By shooting at three officers, both men were capable of murder, but I did not see in either of their faces pure, chilling evil. These were gangbangers who reacted the way they had lived their whole lives: with violence when cornered. They lived their lives on the streets, and while what they did was a horrible crime that changed my life forever, it was not born of pure evil. I looked into their faces many times during that trial and did not see the eyes I had seen before in the murderer from Arkansas and in the juvenile from Battle Creek. The men who tried to kill me had the faces of violent criminals who deserved to rot in prison.

One man who shot at a cop had a face that defined evil. On May 9, 2005, I received the call every officer and their loved ones fear. It was just past four o'clock, and I had just lain down to catch a quick nap before my 10 p.m. shift. Keri was shaking me awake and looked very concerned, "Bran, it's your dad." My dad wasn't one to just randomly call at four o'clock on a week-day to say "Hey." I knew this wasn't good and braced myself for bad news. I had no idea how devastating this news would be as all our lives in the Battle Creek Police Department would be changed forever. "Turn on your TV. Your friend Lavern has been shot." The kind of details that unfolded over the next days is the most difficult that cops have to deal with.

My coworker and good friend Lavern had been shot and killed at the age of forty-seven, leaving behind a wife, Melanie, and two young daughters. He and his partner Greg Huggett were running lead on an investigation into a murder that had been discovered that morning: a jogger spotted an unoccupied but running cab in front of an elementary school. The cabdriver had been stuffed into the trunk, lying in a pool of his own blood. He had been stabbed repeatedly. Detectives began following up on the cabbie's fares for the prior evening, and one of them led to an apartment complex less than a quarter mile from where the cab was found.

As Detectives Huggett and Brann approached the apartment security door they were buzzed in. Both were wearing suits, standard detective dress, but neither wore a bullet-proof vest. This was fairly common practice for any plainclothes assignment. In the culture of police work, wearing a vest just hasn't been done. Most of a detective's work occurs in an interview room at the police station and in a courtroom. When working the street, detectives often do not transition to a vest such as that worn on patrol. This custom has begun to shift, though, toward a more officer-safety approach as critical incidents continue to occur with devastating results.

As Lavern walked toward the apartment door on May 9, 2005, the door swung open and he was confronted by a shotgun-wielding suspect. The first shot struck him in the chest and the second in Detective Huggett's leg. The suspect fled from the wounded detectives, as Lavern fought for his life. Unfortunately, his fight was no match for the damage the shotgun slug had done to his heart. He passed away that afternoon, another hero in blue, doing what he loved to protect us all. There is not a day we don't think about him. I know many officers who have lost their friends on the job, and they all say the same thing: "Man, I wish you had known him" or "She was one hell of a good cop." If you had known Vern, you'd have said it too. We miss him every day.

After the murder of the cabdriver and then Lavern, a manhunt ensued. Every available officer worked to locate the suspect. We worked all day and night combing every street and alley. We were all so angry. That's the closest I came as a cop to wanting vengeance. It felt as though we wanted to find this man and kill him. I'm not saying that is what would have happened. I like to believe in retrospect that we would have been the professionals that we are, that we would have just arrested him and left him to the maze of the legal system. If I'm being truly honest, though, I'm not sure that if we'd found him that night, he would be alive. But we didn't.

The suspect randomly hijacked a car from a random couple driving near the edge of town. He pointed a gun in the driver's face and stole the car. The suspect then drove over a hundred miles east of Battle Creek to Dearborn, Michigan. He was arrested later that night after a car chase and standoff with Dearborn police. After he was found competent to stand trial, he was convicted of murder and will spend the rest of his life in prison without the possibility of parole.

The true face of evil is rarely seen by even those in law enforcement. But when they see it, that face is never forgotten. That's when we go home, kiss our children, tuck them into bed, and thank God they're safe for one more night.

10

FAMILY AND
BACKPACKING

Every police officer has a family: the ones waiting for you
to come home at the end of a shift. The most important
people in our lives. For me, that was my precious wife,
Kerianne, and our two sons, three-year-old Jordan and two-
year-old Zachary. I first met Kerianne at our high school, Grand
Rapids Christian High. She had the most beautiful smile, and I
couldn't keep my eyes off her whenever I saw her in the hallway
between classes. But because I was then an immature teenager,
she was not into me or my partying friends. We never dated, and
she moved on to Calvin College to become a social worker. But
fate entered my life when a couple years later Kerianne called
me, asking if I wanted to go to a wedding for a mutual friend
of ours from high school. It was great to hear her voice after
not seeing her for several years, and I readily agreed to go. We
had a great time, and one date led to two and the rest is history.
We were married on September 25, 1992, one of the happiest

days of my life. I married far above the type of girl with whom I imagined myself being, and she has been my rock throughout our life together.

We come to the profession bringing with us those we care about the most. Officers come from all walks of life. We have different ethnicities, different interests, different spiritual views, different goals, and different dreams. But most of us come into the first years on the job starting a family of our own, and those we care for the most are the ones we return to every day after our shift. They're also the ones we leave behind every day. This is not intentional. But if other police officers look at my own example, they may feel as though they are looking in a mirror.

Kerianne moved to Battle Creek with me when I became an officer with the BCPD. She quickly got a job working for Calhoun County Community Mental Health. She was a great social worker and often my job would cross hers in various mental-health cases. She worked first shift, and because I was newer I worked second shift, so I would see her at home either before she went to bed or in the morning if I got up earlier. Because I had lower seniority, my days off were on Mondays and Tuesdays, so I worked weekends when she had her days off. There was the ever-present temptation to work overtime and either pull double shifts or work on my days off, which I often did.

Many young couples who are not involved in law enforcement find themselves in situations like this. Many factory and other jobs have shift work, leaving couples in similar circumstances in which they say hi in passing. Every couple must learn to adjust to these situations and work on their relationship. Shifts get better over time, and eventually with seniority a balance is struck that works for your family.

But with police work comes a silent threat that is working against all officers and their families, and it was one that I never saw coming. It flies under the radar so much that I will have to explain it. I didn't understand it until years later, when former BCPD officer turned psychologist Bill "Heff" Heffernan explained it to me. Police officers come to the job with a family of some kind, whether married or not. Because they're generally young, newer cops begin their careers and often start their families at about the same time. These are the people we fell in love with and cared so much for that we made them the closest people in our lives. These are also the people with whom we share our closest thoughts, secrets, dreams, and fears. They are the people we trust most.

Our police work is exciting at first, but we begin to see things that are so traumatic and difficult to deal with, things that the average person outside our world will likely never see. Unless they were a soldier in a war, most people will not see things like shootings, stabbing injuries, a child decapitated in a car accident, or someone burned to death in a fire. They won't see the brutality of rape or abuse of the elderly. They won't smell death in a body's many phases of decomposition. They won't feel the fear of rounding dark hallways with your weapon drawn to search for an armed and dangerous suspect. They won't witness countless cases of child abuse and neglect. They won't be spit on or called names simply for being in a uniform. They won't watch their partner become seriously injured or die on the job. Whether handling a serious matter or a simple car accident, a police officer is dealing with problems that most citizens will never experience.

Then, each day after their shift, newer officers return home. They may choose to share some of what they experienced with their loved ones, but bit by bit officers begin to hold more in because they feel that either they're protecting their families from the negativity of the job or they just don't feel their loved ones will understand. This doesn't happen overnight.

73

In fact, I started out telling Keri everything about my job and what I had experienced that day. But as the first few years passed something else started happening. I became closer to my family in blue and realized how much they experienced the same negativity and traumas on the job. I started going out for a drink after the shift to decompress from the shift and rehash it with the crew I had just worked with. Of course, that meant a phone call to Keri letting her know I'd be out and telling her "Good night. I love you." If I saw her the next morning or evening, she would always ask, "How was your day?" The more I was able to decompress with other officers, the more I would tell her it was fine. I didn't mean any harm; I just didn't want to share it with her that day.

I didn't go out to a bar after every shift to wind down. There certainly are many officers who do, but I genuinely loved going home to and being with Kerianne. I just found that as the weeks turned into months, and the months into years, I didn't want to tell her what I had seen on the job. Some of the more traumatic things would come weeks apart or in waves. Yet I was finding that I started just keeping things to myself and telling her that I was fine.

Heff taught me that there is ultimately a cost for taking baggage from our job and stuffing it away inside. He said that all cops have a backpack, and into it go all the things we don't process, thinking we'll deal with it later or not at all. This backpack grows slowly over time, and the heavier it gets the more it will demand attention at some point. Opening up a cop's backpack after decades of filling it is not an easy thing to do. Many require, as I did eventually, professional help in dealing with all that comes out of that backpack. Each cop has a backpack, whether we like it or not.

The decompression I had been going through with other cops was not helping relieve the steady stress of the job either.

I thought that if I could have a half-dozen beers or more and chatted with my coworkers, I could talk out the crap we were all seeing and coping with. That's one of the biggest lies in our profession. Going to a bar and talking to other officers meant I wasn't dealing with anything I was stuffing away. Why is it that actually talking about our day or night wasn't analogous to going to a psychologist's office? Getting cops to tell you that they even believed in psychology is a rarity. Still, why wouldn't talking to fellow officers be the same thing? After I had participated in decades of this self-therapy, you'd think the answer would have hit me sooner. The difference never occurs to most cops until near the end of their career at the soonest, and more likely never.

The reason is simple and infinitely complicated at the same time: no matter how much cops talk to each other—or others, for that matter—about the job, they never talk about how the job makes them *feel* and how it truly *affects* them. Heff taught me this years later when I was so messed up inside that I was no longer capable of processing my feelings; I had kept them pent up for so many years. No matter how many sessions I had had in a bar after my shifts, I never told my closest friends in blue how I felt. Why hadn't I been able to do that? Why couldn't I share my feelings with those who meant the most to me? Every day we are tasked with a job that requires confidence, bravery, and even a certain edge. We start to feel that we have no fear of anything and that any showing of emotion is a sign of weakness. We'd think that officer wasn't fit to do the job. This cycle of bravado never ceases and in fact stays with all officers their entire career. It's part of the blue family's culture.

I remember tipping beers and discussing how some rookie had "blown chunks" at a recent homicide scene, because he couldn't handle the smell of the body and the gore of the gaping hole in the victim's head. We howled in laughter at the weakness that the rookie had displayed, but we conceded that he was a rookie and it was a rite of passage to have something like that shock him.

But what if a death investigation caused a five-year officer to throw up? There would be relentless gossipy discussions by fellow officers about how weak that officer is not to be able to stomach the scene and whether he could handle the job. This atmosphere of bravado only gets worse when you start talking about officers feeling fear on the job. Many times I felt fear to the point where I didn't sleep well for weeks. But to talk about that with another officer? No chance in hell. So, stuff it in the backpack. Again and again and again.

By the time I had passed my fifth or sixth year, I was well into a routine that was slowly sucking the air out of my marriage. I would work as much as I could, and I communicated less and less to Keri about what my job was like. She was still the girl I fell in love with, though. I remembered times in those first ten years of work when I would go away on vacation and then return to those feelings and reasons why I cared for her in the first place. It seemed that if you got away from police work for a period of time, you could almost forget the stress that clouded your vision. Except each year I was becoming more and more callous and less able to laugh. I was becoming a harder person on the inside and rarely showed my feelings. I was never a person to cry much, but during this transition I can remember going to many funerals at which I just stood there with a blank expression on my face incapable of emotion.

To qualify: it is not all bad that police officers, as they mature and become veterans, start to close off their emotions. This is both a defense mechanism and a necessity for officers to survive on the job long-term. They cannot be emotional wrecks call after call and expect to even make it through a year. In fact, officers who are the quietest and have twenty years on the job are the ones least likely to exhibit any sense of panic when the shit hits the fan.

The problem for officers is not their hard exteriors but their hardened interiors. If officers can't tell anyone how they feel about what they are experiencing, then they will fill a backpack whether they like it or not. That backpack will begin to fill, will spill over at some point, and will force officers to confront their problems. Depending on officers' careers, their experiences and personal lives will determine how they handle their overstuffed backpack. Some of us will never deal with it and will continue to self-medicate.

In writing about my experiences, I don't expect every cop to agree with me. I'm relaying only what I have learned in my life on the job and hoping some of it might help. But Heff told me he was seeing cops as patients from all over Michigan, some driving from as far away as Detroit. He couldn't keep up with the demand he was getting from so many cops, each one with a complicated, overstuffed backpack.

Keri and I nearly got divorced as I entered my seventh year at BCPD. She worked the first shift, I mainly worked the second and third shifts, and all of this was taking its toll. Then I had taken on additional assignments as a member of the Emergency Tactical Response Team, had to carry a pager, and had to be ready to respond on all days and at all times, including pass days. This team dealt with crises such as barricaded gunmen with hostages. I have not-so-fond memories of our entire family or a group of friends at our house, steaks on the grill, and the whine of the pager going off signaling another emergency.

I have to be fair, though. Keri never complained about my duties as an officer. She knew what she had signed up for in marrying a cop and admitted as much. That's not what led us to the brink of divorce. Instead it was my failure to communicate how I felt about anything that started cracking the foundation of a once-strong relationship. I couldn't have seen it coming either.

I had become a hardened person inside and carried that over into my personal life. Years of what I had seen and done were taking a toll on me and the person I loved the most. But I wasn't alone.

Statistics are all over the map on how high the divorce rate is for police officers. I would wager an educated guess that it's higher than the national average, after watching many of my fellow officers and their broken relationships. The rate of divorce is not the point, though. It's the *cause* of all the divorces in law enforcement that is the point. I certainly do not profess to be able to explain why police officers often have difficulty in their personal lives. Outside factors that have nothing to do with police work play a role in many situations. The hardening of an officer's interior can have consequences. Most officers go into the profession blind and find after many years that they are unable to cope with a relationship and the job together.

When I was seriously injured, I had never seen a psychologist about anything. In fact, I really thought the profession of psychology was filled with charlatans preaching bunk science for money. Many officers share this opinion, because it fits with their hardened perspectives on life and their inability to even begin to tell anyone how we feel about much of anything. Why would we believe in psychology? If you're seriously hurt, suck it up and get your ass back to work, right? I mean, a showing of weakness is the beginning of the end for us as cops, so who wants to see a shrink and open up that can of worms? This was the place I too was in mentally as I entered my tenth year on the job.

But for Keri, I would probably be wallowing in another broken relationship, wondering why I couldn't get it right. Looking back, I know that she is the only reason we are not divorced today. She was grounded in faith, she persevered through some rough years during which I ignored her and was not a good husband. I worked long hours and walled myself off emotionally as we trudged through the years. I had no idea how special a person she really was, how much she loved me, until I faced the biggest challenge in my life in September 2000. In fact, many of us don't know how much we really care about each other until we're faced with challenges. Mine was going to change everything for us and define a much different future than the one I had planned, a much different future than the one I thought I could control.

Keri and I with Zachary (2) and Jordan (3), after attending the police memorial and awards ceremonies (May, 2001).

11

SUPERVISION AND COMMUNITY

As I approached the end of my first decade on the job, I decided to make a change in my career path and became a supervisor and a sergeant. I had mixed feelings as several people I knew changed when they were promoted. I had formed great bonds working the road in patrol and knew that if I ever took a supervisory path those bonds would suffer. You have to create distance if you expected to be an effective supervisor. But I was determined to earn respect from the road officers and be someone they could rely on.

I took the test to be a sergeant because I was so disappointed with a few of the supervisors I had worked for. It can be miserable to work for a boss who is an ineffective leader and whom you do not respect. My father taught me that if something really bothered me that much, I shouldn't just bitch about it but rather should change it. So I did. I tested well and was promoted in my eighth year on the job.

I was almost demoted within minutes of being notified that I was promoted to sergeant, and the demotion would have been my fault. I received a letter notifying me of the chief of police's decision to promote me, and he scheduled a meeting in his office in two days. In the meantime, the Fraternal Order of Police golf outing took place on the day I got the letter. It was always a great event, and most officers attended. I was joined up with Officers Brian Sparschu, Kurt Roth, and Randy Reinstine. Although we weren't bad golfers, the game was always secondary to several cold beers. On this particular day we had several, and on the back nine holes of the Riverside Golf Course our golf cart crashed when we drove it down one of the hills at a high rate of speed. The cart's top and side were bent, so we pushed and pulled the frame back into place as best as we could. After our round was over we parked the cart and headed for the clubhouse for dinner. I didn't give the cart a second thought as our repair job was sufficient. At least it seemed so with a few beers in us.

Early the next morning my pager went off. Sergeant Tim Kendall requested that I call him. Sergeant Kendall was an excellent officer who was one of my first supervisors when I joined the Emergency Response Tactical unit. We had been through many critical incidents together, and he had gained the trust of all the officers working under him. When I called him the first words out of his mouth were "What the hell did you guys do to the golf cart yesterday?" I knew instantly that I was in trouble because we hadn't told anyone about the damaged cart. We thought we'd repaired it on our own. Sergeant Kendall explained that golf course personnel had called the brass at the police department and complained that we had damaged the cart to the tune of $250.

That wasn't the worst of it. Apparently, the police commander in charge of the patrol division had decided that because I had failed to notify golf course personnel that we had damaged their cart, he was going to stop my promotion because of my behavior and lack of supervisory judgment. The commander was right. But thanks to Tim's six o'clock in the morning call, I had a small window of opportunity and took it.

When the golf course opened at seven o'clock in the morning, I was at the door. I held a blank check and explained that my friends and I had damaged a golf cart the previous day, and we needed to know what it was going to cost to fix it. The maintenance employee asked me if the commander had sent me, and I replied honestly that he had not. After getting an estimate, I wrote the check, went home, and started doing yard work on my day off.

Within an hour, my pager went off again, and I was summoned to the police chief's office immediately. This meeting was a day earlier than the one scheduled for me to see him about my promotion, but I knew the reason. I saw fixed eyes and deep, funereal frowns on the faces of the commander and the chief. The chief told me to sit down. Not a good start. The commander took over the meeting. He asked me if I had damaged a golf cart. I answered, "Yes, sir." Before I could explain he continued, "And who did you report this damage to?"

I gave him the name of the maintenance employee I had reported to that morning. "Excuse me, Officer. Are you saying that you reported the damage to somebody at the golf course?" Any officer who lies to a command officer is a serious offense, and the commander was certain that I just had. "Please explain," he said, dumbfounded. I told him what I'd done that morning. I could see a wry smile on the chief's face; he knew that I had somehow miraculously gotten out in front of this mess.

The commander was furious. "Who told you to do that?" I didn't lie to the commander or out my source so I skirted the question by responding, "Sir, I knew it was the right thing to do."

He was red-faced and angry but had nothing else to say. After another awkward silence, the chief said, "Nicely done, Officer Hultink. Thank you for taking care of the damaged property. It is obviously very important that we, as representatives of our department, carry ourselves in public a certain way. Especially as supervisors." He raised his eyebrows, and his meaning was crystal clear: I was entering a new phase in my career that required a different level of discretion. The commander looked frustrated and perplexed, but that was the last I heard of the golf course incident or any potential discipline. The next day I was promoted and handed my sergeant's badge. Thank you, Sergeant Tim Kendall.

Being a sergeant is very satisfying and lonely at the same time. On the one hand, you are in charge of a section of the city and handle a large variety of calls. If there is a crisis, you get to manage it and ultimately have a say in what resolution or direction it will take. On the other hand, it can be lonely because the good times you used to have with your fellow road patrol officers fade away as they treat you more like a boss and less like a peer. All this is necessary to being an effective supervisor and leader. But it can be an adjustment after having bonded with a tight-knit group of officers.

I was determined to learn from some of the best supervisors how to navigate this period of adjustment. Over time I learned how to effectively supervise without losing touch with where I had come from, the road. Two people in particular kept me grounded: K-9 Officer Marc Holso and Officer Kurt Dittmer. They candidly spoke to me anytime I started to get too full of myself. Both had a sharp, sarcastic wit and didn't let me get away with anything. We became good friends over the years, and while I may have never told them this, I wouldn't have been half the sergeant I was without their influence.

They helped me understand that the most effective thing a leader can do is to lead from the front. For a sergeant, that meant still showing up on calls for service first and at times relieving a patrol officer of paperwork and doing it yourself. It meant showing officers that I was not afraid to participate in their daily grind and that I would still get into the fray and be a part of their lives. This approach to supervision would ultimately lead me to my first armed confrontation with a suspect.

I was working overtime on afternoon shift as one of the north-side sergeants and heard a call about a shooting by a male suspect and a female victim lying in the front yard. When I got to the area I was met by the driver of an Aaron's Rent-To-Own truck who was in apparent shock; all he could do was point toward the lawn of one of the houses. There I found a woman in her early twenties. Half her face was missing, and she was clearly dead. She had bled out in the yard. Next to her was a shotgun, and without any other information the scene could have looked like a suicide. I returned to the driver and after interviewing him understood why he was so shaken.

He had arrived at the end of the street to repossess some rental property when he noticed a tall man in his twenties arguing profanely with a woman who was around the same age. The driver noticed the man had a shotgun in his hand and as he shoved the woman, he suddenly pointed the shotgun at her head and fired. She was knocked backward and fell to the ground, half her head gone. But the man wasn't finished even though she was dead. The driver said that the man began to kick her side repeatedly as he cursed at her, accusing her of cheating on him. He finally threw the shotgun down next to her body and fled on foot. After officers canvassed neighbors, we discovered who the suspect and the victim were and I had dispatch put out an all-points bulletin to have him arrested.

When a bulletin is put out on a police radio, an entire community of citizens religiously listen with their scanners. They often will call in tips and can be a vital part of solving crimes or finding a missing person. There are also some callers with significant mental-health issues who call in tips that are far from reality. The sergeant and the dispatchers weed out the calls with merit from the many that have none; the latter can unnecessarily sap the time and energy of the police force on duty. Occasionally, some calls are even designed as a diversion to draw police away from a certain area so a suspect can escape or another crime can occur. The process of vetting calls into a dispatch center when a dangerous suspect is on the loose is not an easy one.

Several calls came in over the course of the afternoon indicating that a black male had run through their yard and might be the suspect or a male wearing all dark clothing was in the woods next to their house, and so on. These calls described twenty percent of Battle Creek's population and were not credible enough. People want to help solve crime, and with a dangerous suspect out they want to even more. Unfortunately, the gap between wanting to help and actually making a difference is a large one. So, on this night it was our job as sergeants to sift through call after call and drive through a lot of neighborhoods just in case.

At just before ten o'clock in the evening a call came in naming the suspect and listing an address he was seen entering minutes before. I called several officers together and we approached the residence by having two officers cover the street behind the residence while Detective Adams and I went to the front door. As a newer sergeant, though, I made a mistake. Dave rode with me in my marked patrol car as we approached the residence; I kept my headlights off. My mistake was thinking the suspect wasn't looking out for police, whether the patrol car was dark or not. We carefully parked several doors down from the address where the suspect was purported to be, but as we walked up the front steps to the residence I could hear crashing in the bushes in the backyard. It was clear the suspect was fleeing on foot. One of the officers covering the backstreet saw the suspect running, but it was a congested neighborhood and even with a K-9 track we could not relocate him—he was "in the wind."

As I began my second consecutive eight-hour shift at ten o'clock, several calls were still coming in to the dispatch center and some indicated possible suspect locations and sightings. The calls were vague and did not lead to anything. I was mad at myself for losing such a dangerous suspect with such a sloppy approach when we had had such a good tip. As a tactical officer I knew better and should have had officers closer to the back of the residence when we approached the front door; either that or simply conducted surveillance. As the night wore on I played the failed attempt in my head repeatedly. It's just the kind of thing a supervisor has to deal with: whether something they screwed up could lead to the death or serious injury of another citizen or officer. The burden of command is very real when the stakes are higher, as they were on this night.

Just after one o'clock in the morning a tip came in to the dispatch center that had all the markings of legitimacy. A woman was on the phone whispering that she was hiding in the bathroom of her apartment. She told the dispatcher that she was the ex-girlfriend of the guy we had been looking for, and that he had just come to her apartment unannounced. She said he was acting very strangely, extremely paranoid, and was armed with some type of silver handgun that he kept waving around as he repeatedly checked out the front and back windows. He had told her the police were looking for him, and he was going to crash at her place for the night. He had also told her that if she attempted to leave with her kids, he would kill her. A hostage negotiation was developing, and her call was a very strong lead.

Determined to learn from earlier missteps, I called officers to assist me with approaching the apartment and the potentially armed and dangerous suspect. Sergeant Todd Madsen and Officers Jim Tuyls, Grady Pierce, and Mike Bradley came with me. Todd and I were both supervisors on the tactical team, and I chose to have us park on an adjacent street, walk through the yards in the dark, and stage within about fifty feet of where the caller's back door was. Once we were in place, the officers would turn onto the street and in a marked patrol car drive directly to and approach the residence. The suspect would see the marked police vehicles, and if he chose to run, we had the back covered. If he decided to stay in the house, then we would handle it as a contained critical hostage negotiation. I was later asked why we would place the caller in danger if we knew we might risk making the suspect mad and potentially irrational. It's one of the supervisory decisions in which you're damned if you do and damned if you don't. I felt that the caller was already in danger, and that our plan would successfully draw the suspect out of the residence away from her and the kids. I decided the plan was a go.

Todd and I spent about ten minutes parking our car nearby and worked our way slowly in the dark to our positions of cover behind some trees in the caller's backyard. Once we were in place we radioed the officers to approach the front. As they turned onto the street and drove to within a half block of the front, the back sliding door opened and a man matching the suspect's description poked his head out, looking left and right for any activity in the backyard. Seeing none, he came outside and started running in our direction. When he got within about thirty feet we showed ourselves, both of us in police uniforms, and told him to stop. We announced that we were the police. He was startled, but we could see both of his hands, and he did not appear armed.

Immediately he bolted back toward the apartment, but this time toward the side as if he were going to run to the front. As he was running I could see he was attempting to grab something from his waistband with his right hand. Todd and I simultaneously raised our guns to address the possibility that he might have a weapon, while yelling for him to show both of his hands. All of this was happening in a matter of five or six seconds, and as the suspect approached the corner of the apartment building, he had still not shown us the front waistband where he had his right hand.

When the suspect reached the corner of the building, Todd and I were about fifteen feet behind him and closing in. We started rounding the corner as I noticed the suspect produce a silver handgun from his waistband and start to raise it up away from us in the opposite direction. I was about to pull the trigger and prepare to shoot him if necessary as I followed the direction he was pointing his handgun. In that split second I saw Officer Bradley with the other two officers right behind him. They were rounding the corner at the front of the residence and were almost in our line of fire. I chose not to pull the trigger as my fire would be directly toward the officers. Sergeant Madsen also did not fire his weapon. At that moment, a blast came from a gun with the flare of fire erupting from the barrel. I heard pings of metal on brick to my right against the apartment wall and then heard the suspect exhale in a half wail, half moan as he fell to the ground. I pointed my flashlight toward Officer Bradley, and I saw Mike standing with a shotgun pointed at an angle toward the suspect. I realized that Mike had fired and shot the suspect in the groin, severely injuring him. On the ground next to the suspect's right hand was the silver handgun that he had just pointed at Mike;

I kicked it away from his reach. He was crumpling up in a fetal position and moaning.

We immediately contacted dispatch and requested an ambulance. I then contacted Lieutenant Mike Sherzer, who was in command of the entire city on this evening, and let him know what had happened. An officer-involved shooting sets in motion a lot of moving parts, and Lieutenant Sherzer orchestrated that process. First, he called the chief of police, Jeffrey Kruithoff. Then he contacted Inspector of Internal Affairs Mike Olson. Finally, he called the supervisors of the Detective Bureau, Commander Phil Reed and Sergeant Carter Bright. All of them would be conducting interviews and investigating an event that had lasted only about ten seconds. Every detail of what had happened would be scrutinized, just the way a surgeon's work is analyzed under the microscope of a peer review session of doctors.

Sergeant Madsen made sure the suspect was unarmed and started directing the crime scene. Meanwhile, I took Officer Bradley aside, secured his firearm in my patrol vehicle as evidence, and had him take a seat to decompress. Mike Bradley was a quiet guy most days, but he hadn't said much since the shot had been fired. Everything had escalated so quickly that I think his mind and mine were trying to make sense of what had just happened. This is how a police shooting feels from the side of law enforcement. You don't go out on shift wanting to take somebody's life. You don't go out on shift even wanting to take your gun out of its holster. But in the span of a few seconds an officer is expected to a make a decision that affects lives. It is one of the most difficult jobs in the world for this reason alone.

The suspect was dying, and quickly. He had been shot once with a police-issue twelve-gauge shotgun and was bleeding heavily. He was now completely curled up in a ball, and after another minute the Lifecare paramedics arrived and quickly determined he needed to be moved fast. He was on his way to the hospital in seconds. I headed to the police station with Officer Bradley and met the others in the detective bureau. Sergeant Bright told me the suspect had died upon arriving at the hospital. All of us who had participated in capturing the suspect were now part of a homicide investigation. We would all be interviewed extensively, and the county prosecutor would determine whether the homicide was justifiable or not. After several months we were finally told that Mike's actions as a shooter and our actions as a team were justified under the circumstances, making it a justifiable homicide. During that time Mike was placed on paid administrative leave and had to wait for someone in an office to tell him that his actions, completed in a few seconds, were the right ones.

I was right there in the middle of the situation, and I can assure you that not only were the actions justified, but the officers were courageously brave under difficult circumstances. I often think of this shooting incident when I see stories of how police reacted under equally difficult circumstances. Today we are living in times unlike any other when it comes to police scrutiny. Police officers are put through the gauntlet of public opinion on issues such as community relations, use of force, and high-speed chases. At the same time, the tax-paying public expects a perfect police force to respond at a moment's notice to its every need.

The toxic relationship that existed between the police and the citizens of Ferguson, Missouri, did not happen overnight. It festered over a long time and was swept under the rug until it boiled over after the controversial shooting of Michael Brown on August 9, 2014. The community, even the nation, took one police incident in a small town in Missouri and made it a symbol for police conduct everywhere. In my generation, the same thing was done when officers clearly acted outside the law and proper use of force in the beating of Rodney King in Los Angeles,

California, on March 3, 1991. I can clearly remember working the streets as a young officer during those years and citizens yelling at me, "What're you gonna do, beat me like you did Rodney?"

Police officers are not perfect and will make mistakes, just as people in the community are not perfect and will also screw up sometimes. What is important is that any police force must foster a positive, inclusive, and cooperative relationship with its citizens of all races and backgrounds. This cannot just be a show for the cameras. It must be a meaningful, involved process in which all points of view are heard and acted on. In any police shooting there are strong feelings on both sides. The police are angry because they were placed in danger and had to take a life. They could have even lost police lives or suffered severe injury themselves. The public is angry because the police have once again had to shoot a citizen in their community. Some support police actions. But in a shooting in which a police officer is perceived to have used excessive force, the public may turn the other way.

Then there is the volatile issue of race. Having been a career cop, I think that most cops only see blue. But I have also learned that each of us brings our unique experiences and backgrounds to the job. Some of us grew up rich and some poor. Some of us are black and some white. Some of us are male and some female. Some are Christian, some are Muslim, some are Jewish, some are of other religions or no religion at all. The diversity we bring to the job is what makes us great and is also what makes us human. Within that humanity, though, we have to step back and accept that we're not perfect. We need to learn to be tactically effective, well-trained officers who engage as partners in the communities we serve

The best example of this is drugs. All veteran cops will tell you that policing drugs in any community through arrest and detention is a losing battle. The drugs will always show up, and the addicts and associated crimes just keep coming. We need to create partnerships to address the problem, and police are finding that community members want to be involved in making where they live better. The police are getting better in how they approach and communicate with their citizens, instead of just shaking them down on a street corner just because they're a certain race or age. In turn the community starts identifying the problem dealers by name, and information is more streamlined. Community centers are started for addiction, and people start to turn corners in their lives. Yes, the drugs will still be there, but slow it all down and a community in partnership with its cops can make huge strides. This is the conversation that needs to start taking place so that we don't just stop people based on how they look. This is the conversation that needs to start taking place so that we don't become Ferguson, Missouri.

12

SEPTEMBER 25, 2000

By fall 2000, I was working nights as one of three sergeants covering the city. I had started attending Thomas M. Cooley Law School and almost completed my first of four years. I had developed a fairly normal routine. School from six o'clock to nine o'clock in the evening, then drive to work and cover nights from ten o'clock in the evening until six o'clock in the morning. After that, get some sleep and wake up and get ready for class. If there was any free time, I'd try to squeeze in something with the family. My goal was to get my law degree and move up the ranks of supervision. During this first year of law school, I was so busy that Keri and I were more like brother and sister than spouses. She was supportive and essentially started raising Zachary and Jordan by herself. I often look back on those years with regret that I missed so much as they grew from babies to bustling and busy boys.

I woke up on September 25, 2000, with a bad chest cold. Law school and all the hours at work were beginning to take a toll. It was about seven o'clock in the evening, and I had already decided to skip class that night to get the extra sleep. I felt like crap and was beginning the internal discussion of whether I should call in sick or not. The truth was, I was taking too many days off for school already just to study for my final exams. I needed to go to work, but calling in and climbing back under the covers would feel so good. Keri knew me well, and without my having to say anything she confronted me with "You're not gonna call in sick, are you?" That made me laugh and start a fit of coughing. I knew she was right, and after another few hours of studying, I got dressed and headed into work.

It was a night like any other, starting with the evening briefing in our lineup room. My fellow sergeants, Dave Walters and Todd Madsen, and I read the material to the officers and after about fifteen minutes started the shift. It was a colder fall night, and temperatures were falling into the upper forties. This meant a promising night for low call volume and likely a good one to get some studying done for school. The warmer the weather, the more calls and violence erupt in the city. This night looked like a quiet one.

As the shift progressed, it was as slow as anticipated. By two in the morning I don't think we had gotten even ten calls, none of them significant. I had gotten a few hours of reading done and headed back to the station to kill some more time in the sergeant's office with Dave and Todd. We got some paperwork done and talked for a while. Then at around three in the morning a call came in about shots fired in the Washington Heights neighborhood. This was a common type of call that came in almost nightly in the city and certainly wasn't cause for alarm. Most often, officers would simply check the area for anything unusual and then contact the dispatcher, letting him or her know they were available and back in service.

Todd and I decided to double up and ride in one patrol car together, advising dispatch that we would respond to the area.

Along with us, Patrol Officer Tom Rivera also responded in a separate vehicle. As we approached the address of the caller, 417 Parkway Drive, I noticed a man waving at us from the porch. At this point nothing seemed unusual, and in most calls like this we would simply get the name of the complainant and clear back into service, having seen nothing related to the original shots-fired call. I got out of the patrol car along with Todd and noticed Tom Rivera arriving on the other side of the street as well. The three of us walked up the driveway together.

I noticed that the caller had parked his red minivan in the front yard of his residence, a parking violation. He was well known by the night-shift officers as an early-morning paper deliveryman using that red van with the yellow lights on top. It appeared he had cleared his driveway of broken concrete and was getting ready to have it repaved. As we walked up the driveway, I noticed a black van parked in the driveway adjacent to the caller's. It was parked facing the road and had tinted windows with the words "Washington Heights Church" on the side. Despite being parked in a residential driveway, it didn't look out of place because we were in the Washington Heights neighborhood. We walked farther up the driveway toward the caller, and then I heard noise coming from the van. It sounded to me like scraping or shuffling on metal. I told Todd and Tom that "there's something in that van."

I had no idea what lay in wait for us inside that van, no idea that about ten minutes before our arrival, three suspects, Ernest Brooks, Deshaun Witcher, and Milo Fitzpatrick, had backed the van into the driveway of the empty lot adjacent to 417 Parkway. They then donned masks and cut south through the backyards on Parkway Drive to a house on Somerset Street, where an after-hours party was in full swing. Armed with two AK-47 assault rifles and a 9-mm handgun equipped with an extended magazine, they entered the side door of the garage where the party was being held and fired numerous rounds into the ceiling. Witnesses later reported the suspects yelled for everyone to lie on the floor while they took the money from the gambling tables, roughly $15,000. Then they left as quickly as they had appeared and slipped back into the darkness of the backyards, arriving back at the van on Parkway Drive and getting inside. What they didn't count on was having the resident of 417 Parkway contact the dispatch center with a call of shots fired somewhere close to his house. He was up early getting ready to go out and deliver newspapers. The dispatch center quickly relayed his information to on-duty officers, and we responded, although we didn't know what had actually taken place.

When I told my fellow officers what I had heard in the van, I was facing it with my flashlight illuminating the tinted windows. I saw an orange flash of light, and my body twisted as I slammed into the ground. I remember feeling a stabbing pain in the left side by my hip, and I was spitting out dirt. I heard two popping sounds over my head and turned to look up, still seeing the reddish orange flashing from the front two windows. All this occurred in the first few seconds.

Years and years of training go into how police officers handle a call in which they are in the middle of a shooting, or worse yet are themselves injured during a shooting. This training often goes unused in a police career. I was well trained, having spent several years working on the Emergency Response Team as a tactical officer and later as a supervisor. This training was vital to what happened in the moments that followed.

As I turned to look up at the van, realizing simultaneously that I was shot and in a firefight, I removed my 40-caliber handgun and fired several rounds at the van's window toward the flashing lights that came from the center window. This is called *suppressive fire* and is critical to winning any firefight, especially one in which you are exposed without any cover.

I remember my initial thoughts were that what I was shooting at, the only thing besides the flashing lights I saw, was the devil. That thought would be significant later on. After I had fired three or four shots, I tried to move, and horror gripped me as I realized I couldn't move my legs. I was paralyzed. I had never felt more helpless in my life, but in that moment there was no time to dwell on it. I fired another couple rounds toward the van and suddenly felt myself being choked and dragged at the same time. I still couldn't move my legs but saw them dragging behind me as I was pulled behind the original caller's red van by Officer Rivera. He had bravely pulled me to a position of cover behind the parked van, while Sergeant Madsen also bravely drew the suspect's fire toward himself as he moved to a separate position of cover behind one of the patrol cars. Both sides exchanged heavy gunfire.

I grabbed my radio and contacted dispatch: "Officer down, I've been shot, officer down." I heard nothing in response and called them again, repeating the statement. Still nothing. What I didn't know at the time is that the bullet, a 7.62 mm fired from an AK-47 assault rifle, had initially struck my police radio, damaging it. The bullet then struck my hip and tore through my midsection. Because a bullet's lead is hot when it enters the body, it was tearing up my insides and simultaneously cutting, burning, and crushing nerves in my legs. Any surgeon will tell you the damage just one bullet can do to the inside of a person. The pain struck me again in a wave. I screamed out "Fuuuuuuuuuuuuuuuck!" several times. About ten seconds had elapsed since the first shot was fired. I noticed the suspect or suspects still firing from the van, and I returned more rounds, emptying my magazine. I was still under the caller's parked van when I saw the other van leave the driveway and crash into a patrol car while leaving the area.

The exchange of almost a hundred rounds was finally over. I turned on my back, and pain slammed into me again.

I looked up at Rivera, and he looked worried. He was ripping off my shirt and vest and finally found where the bullet had struck. I remember writhing in pain. I was beyond yelling profanity at this point, and the pain was so overwhelming that I just flung myself back and forth, moaning. Oddly, I distinctly remember the smell of fresh-cut grass and dew on my cheeks. Investigators are learning more about how people remember things in severe trauma incidents and how they use all of their senses. If you had asked me then if I remember smelling anything, I don't know if I'd have recalled it, but the memory is there. I also remember seeing the fear on Tom's and Todd's faces and hearing them plead for me to hang in there. That scared me. I have never felt fear like this, before or since. I believed that I was going to die. I know I didn't want to die. But I was getting very cold and fading toward unconsciousness. I felt that if I passed out, I wasn't going to wake up.

I remember telling them "I can't feel my legs" several times. I also remember saying "Tell Keri I love her." I believed I wasn't going to make it. That doesn't mean I didn't want to live. But I was in severe pain and getting very cold and weak. I was losing blood from internal bleeding and shock. I didn't see any tunnel of light, but I knew that the way my body felt, coupled with the fact that it was a bullet, meant I was likely going to die. I remember telling Tom, "I'm fading, brother, I'm really fading." I can only imagine the fear and worry they were feeling when their fellow officer told them that, right after the stress and adrenaline of what we had all been through. Those guys fought hard to keep me awake until the ambulance and fire rescue units could arrive. I remember Todd screaming into his radio to get the ambulance there quicker.

When the paramedics arrived, I was very cold, the pain had gone from mind-numbing to almost a dull ache because I was so far gone in shock. It had only been minutes since I was shot, but it felt like hours. I was in such fear of dying that I had completely forgotten that I couldn't move my legs. Once I was in the ambulance, I grabbed on to the shirt of paramedic Christine Robinson and, as scared as I've been in my entire life, asked her, "Am I going to die?" The look on her face told me everything I needed to know. She was worried, and any cop will tell you that a worried paramedic usually means a fatality. Christine was and is married to Matt Robinson, a fellow BCPD officer and good friend who had worked on the tactical team with me for years. It was not fair of me to ask her a question like that, but I was beyond such considerations as I was gripped with fear bordering on terror. Here I was, facing that moment that cops talk about all the time, not really believing they'll ever face such a scenario.

When you're looking right into the face of death, you are forced to deal with something that all of us talk about: Is there an afterlife? Is there something after death? Some people die suddenly, when, for example, they drive a small car head-on into a semi. For them, there is no thought and reflection. For some of us, death comes over a longer period, giving us the ability to contemplate extensively. I believe those who experience the lengthy, drawn out march toward a finality perhaps face the most difficult ending.

As the ambulance sped along the short route from the scene on Parkway Drive to the hospital, death was all I could think about. What if I didn't make it? Will it be like the scene in the movie *Ghost*, in which demons drag the guy's spirit body to hell? That fear of what comes next is very real, and I had not been a very good Christian. Did that mean I wasn't going to get into heaven? These thoughts raced into and out of my head. (In chapter 16, I'll talk about how my faith impacted this moment in the ambulance and my life afterward.) But having stood on the cliff's edge facing death, I felt that there is an afterlife in heaven or in hell. I can't prove it, but if you've ever been to the edge, you can feel it. You know that it's real and that we aren't just something formed from rocks crashing into each other. There is a creator God, who will judge us one day whether we like it or not. If we believe that he sent his son Jesus Christ to die for our sins, then we can be forgiven and, yes, have eternal life with him.

The question I faced as the ambulance pulled into the bay was whether I had truly, in all my hardened, cynical doubt as a cop, believed all that God had done for me. Was I a true believer? I liked to tell people I was, but I also liked to ask them how a God of love could let a child suffer abuse from a molester. As I stood on the edge of my life, I did not feel the assurance of eternal life. All I felt was terror, and one of my last thoughts as I entered the emergency room was whether this was how the people felt as the water started climbing up to their waists after they had mocked Noah for building a boat. Were the years of cynicism as a cop going to result in my eternal damnation? Or would I still be accepted into heaven? My stomach was filling up with blood, and I was barely conscious as we arrived at the hospital.

As I was wheeled into the ER, my pain was being eased by copious amounts of morphine, greatly increasing my fears. I remember seeing Officer Kurt Roth and joking with him. I kept asking Dr. Volkel, whom cops respected as an excellent ER doctor, if things were looking good for me because I felt great. I saw fear on his face and knew I was in trouble. I asked for "Smitty," a day-shift cop named Dan Smith, to come there, and I also kept asking for Keri. I'd find out later that Officers Tim Kendall and Pat Johnson had woken Keri up and driven her to the ER within fifteen minutes of my being shot, allowing her to talk to me before I went into a life-or-death surgery. I will always be grateful to them. When Keri arrived, she was in an obvious state of fear. However, I was on so much morphine by this point that I was smiling and saying, "Hi, honey, I feel great! It's going to be just fine! I'll see you in a few; this is only going to take a few minutes," as they took me into surgery. The morphine replaced all my fear and doubts about eternity, and the last thing I remember is the line of officers in the hallway as I was whisked past them. Each grabbed my hand or shoulder as I went by. That is the brotherhood of blue.

What the doctors and I did not know at this point was that the bullet had cut the iliac vein in my left leg, which caused me to slowly but consistently bleed internally. I had filled up with so much blood, and my blood pressure had dropped so significantly, that Dr. Volkel later told me he almost opened me up in the ER. Dr. Volkel was a veteran of the Vietnam War, and as a MASH surgeon, he was considered one of the better ER surgeons in our area. He also was one of the few doctors who always had a police scanner on while he was working night shift. He told me it was an old habit from the war days when he would monitor military channels for incoming wounded. On this night, his police scanner played a pivotal role in saving my life. When the shooting call first came out, Dr. Volkel paged Dr. Brian Kozarski, a well-respected surgeon. Those minutes he saved allowed Dr. Kozarski to arrive at the hospital just a few minutes after I was rushed in.

Of course I remember nothing about the surgery but later was given every detail by Officer Ken Milliken, who was present should anything of evidentiary value needed to be collected. Can you imagine being Officer Milliken, who five and a half hours earlier had listened to me give the shift briefing and was now witnessing my surgery?

This was not a typical surgery because Dr. Kozarski had to remove many organs and intestines to search for the source of the bleeding. That required him to tape them outside my body, leaving me a living carcass while the doctor removed bone fragments. Ken later told me he could see my spine, and it looked much like a deer carcass. The cop in me figured that had to be pretty amazing to see. At the same time, it had to be pretty scary for Ken to see a fellow cop in surgery. It took a meticulous search by Dr. Kozarski to find and tie off the bleed, which required two full blood transfusions. Because of my rare blood type, they had to have blood flown by helicopter from a neighboring city to the hospital mid-surgery. Thanks to a lot of people—on-scene officers, paramedics, firefighters, nurses, and doctors—my life was spared. But I feel that something much bigger than human hands spared me that day.

13

INTENSIVE CARE

I awoke gripped in terror in the middle of the shooting incident. Shots were being fired, I couldn't move, and I reached up and grabbed . . . Jason? Confusion was all I could muster as I lay there in a cold sweat trying to figure out why I was covered in all kinds of wires with a tube in my throat, while my cousin Jason was sitting next to me holding my hand. Jason, or JJ, was one of my best friends, and while I couldn't figure out why he was there, I was glad to see him. He calmly used a writing pad to explain to me that I was in the Intensive Care Unit (ICU) and that I had just had surgery within the last twenty-four hours. I couldn't believe most of what he was telling me. I knew I was shot, but I couldn't understand why this damned tube was jammed down my throat. Then I felt the pain again in my lower torso and after some more morphine fell back to sleep.

I woke up several more times while Jason was there. Each time I was filled with fear and confusion. Tubes, machines, and wires all hooked up to you will do that. I was clearly a mess to look at, and having Jason there helped me through those initial hours. Not many people were allowed to be in the room, including family. I was still in critical condition and apparently not out of the woods. Doctor after doctor came into and went out of the room, checking the computers, wires, and my chart. I was glad when I went to sleep because the pain was almost unbearable throughout my torso, and came in powerful waves. I couldn't move without experiencing pain so bad that it immediately brought tears to my eyes. It was all I could do to just try to lie still and hope the pain medication would help, but nothing did. Keri told me they were giving me the maximum amount they could, given my critical condition. I just kept scribbling on the scratch paper to give me more.

When my condition had stabilized a little, Inspector Mike Olson and Commander Neal Vanderbilt came to take my statement. It was a slow process, but suspects were still at large and information was important. One of the details I gave them was that when the suspects initially shot at me, I saw the devil. Investigators discounted this detail as something inaccurate in the heat of the battle. This detail hurt the credibility of my entire recollection of events. The issue of *victim's traumatic recollection* is something that we police are still learning about today. Often victims of severe and sudden trauma remember specific details that we need to take into account. What were they feeling, seeing, smelling, hearing, and even tasting? All of our senses are heightened during the traumatic event, and investigators today are learning much more, which leads to more comprehensive investigations and results.

I spent the next two days in the ICU, most of it asleep. Then they transferred me to a regular hospital bed, my home for the next two weeks. It was very early in the morning and dark outside, but I found myself awake mainly because my body was still operating on a third-shift schedule. I had just hit the red button to signal a nurse. Keri was in the corner sleeping in a chair, and I just wanted something to stop the incredible pain. The nurse came in and gave me some Vicodin, which did not help at all. I slowly watched the darkness turn to light as dawn approached. The clock read just past five o'clock.

Into the room walked Dr. Hlavac, one of the neurosurgeons at Battle Creek Health Systems. He quietly flipped through my chart, noticed I was awake, and said, "Good morning." Keri began to wake up. Dr. Hlavac checked my heart rate and the breathing tube, which was still down my throat and preventing my ability to talk. He said that I was lucky to be alive and that the surgery had gone well. I scribbled a question for him on my notepad: How soon would I be able to get back on my feet and back to work? Thus far nobody had told me the extent of my injuries. Dr. Hlavac simply looked at me and in a monotone said, "Son, you are paralyzed from the waist down and will never walk again. You will be lucky if you are able to return to work. The rest will be up to you." He jotted something in my chart and left the room. I was stunned and crushed at the same time. Not able to walk again. Those words kept repeating themselves in my head. Along with the word "paralyzed." It was so final, so damned certain. Three days ago I was training for a triathlon and now this. It was too much for me to comprehend. He left me in tears.

I couldn't even look Keri in the eye as she put her hand on my shoulder. She knew what this meant to me and that it was devastating. She knew not to say anything and to just be there. It's one of the reasons I love her so much. I finally looked at her through tear-filled eyes and said, "Keri, I can't do this. I won't be able to deal with this." She knew what I was talking about and didn't address it. I didn't say anything else for a long time as the minutes turned into an hour and the bustle of the day shift started to pick up in the hallway as the hospital came to life. I was a shell of myself mentally and just wanted to pull the blankets over my head and tune the world out.

But in walked a nurse I had not met yet. She told me that she was going to remove the catheter I had and would be teaching me how to use a straight catheter. I couldn't believe what the hell I was hearing. A what?! Again, I looked at Keri and just shook my head, telling her, "No fucking way am I doing this, Keri." My eyes filled with tears again, and I asked the nurse to give me five minutes, which she did. Keri took my hand in hers and said, "I'll be there with you through all of this, no matter where it takes us." I just looked at her, still shaking my head.

But I never forgot those words. It was something I have never forgotten to this day and was what I needed to hear at that exact moment from the person I loved the most. What was it in our vows: in sickness and in health? Well, the sickness part was going to test us, and I could see that it was starting with a vengeance as soon as that nurse returned. I felt not only pain but also a mixture of frustration and anger. I thought, "Why couldn't I just have died out there on the streets, as a hero in a blaze of glory in the firefight?" I just lay back in the bed and tried to move my legs or wiggle my toes. Nothing. I really was paralyzed.

This time the nurse was more determined to complete her task: "Okay, I know, Brandon, that this is not what you wanted to see happen, but due to the level of trauma you have in your midsection, you currently have what we call a neurogenic bladder. This means you can't urinate on your own, and you can't control your ability to urinate. So, you'll need a device called a 'straight catheter' to assist you. I'm going to show you how this is done, but first we're going to remove the hospital catheter you've had in."

Once she removed the more permanent catheter, the nurse produced a package and removed a thin plastic tube with an orange end: a straight catheter. She started explaining the process to Keri and me, and I just tuned her out while still in a state of denial and unbelief. I knew the gist of how this was going to work. Every time I had to pee I was going to have to ram that plastic tube into my pecker and then my bladder would work, abracadabra. Things were just getting worse.

Because the pain was so bad I could barely sit up. I had learned that my pelvis had been shattered and I had extensive nerve damage. Over several hours Dr. Kozarski had patched together shattered bone, and burned and torn nerves and nerve endings. The bullet had torn through the part of the human body where all of the muscles, nerves, and major bones come together to give us mobility and balance. When that area is damaged, the initial pain is nearly unbearable. Every time a doctor or nurse came into the room I asked for pain medication. I was finding it difficult to sleep more than an hour without waking up to pain that felt like somebody had stuck a knife in my side and was constantly twisting it. All they were giving me was Percocet and Vicodin, neither of which was touching the pain. Apparently morphine was now off the menu.

I drifted back to the lengthy explanation the nurse was giving me about how to use the straight catheter—wash your hands a lot, risk of infection, yada yada yada. This was going to really suck. What I had to do was use this lubricant on the end of the catheter and then guide it into my penis until it reached the flap of muscle that entered the bladder. People can normally control that muscle; when they're urinating they just open it and empty the bladder. Now, with my newly acquired neurogenic bladder I was unable to physically open the flap. My bladder would then fill up until it was so full it would burst that flap open, and I would involuntarily urinate. Thankfully, I could feel when my bladder was getting full, so the straight catheter allowed me to live without needing to have a permanent one inserted. I finally was able to figure out how the straight catheter worked and emptied my bladder into a plastic jar while sitting up in bed. It was painful, but not as bad as I thought it would be. I clearly had much less feeling in my groin than before the injury. I was instantly struck with a thought that had not occurred to me, and it filled me with fear and dread. I asked the nurse, "Am I able to have an erection because of my injury?"

The nurse was an older lady who had worked the halls of this hospital for nearly thirty years. The things she had seen and done in her service to others had added wrinkles to the corners of her eyes along with a firm expression and demeanor that just exuded experience. She was the nurse you always hoped you'd have when you went to the hospital, one with confidence and the ability to handle your problems and worries. She sat down on the edge of the bed; she realized she was dealing with someone who was adjusting to another type of life, someone who didn't comprehend all of the changes that lay ahead. She had been here before, maybe not with an injured police officer, but she had been here.

The nurse put her hand on my knee and patted it, although I couldn't feel anything. She told me it was too soon to tell what would and wouldn't work in my midsection and groin. She explained that the trauma and swelling would take weeks, even months, to subside. Then the doctors would have a better handle on what was truly irreparable and what could come back with therapy and healing. I had the feeling that her prognosis was dire, but I still heard the wisdom in her explanation. She said that a neurogenic bladder could get better over time; even a straight catheter might no longer be necessary. It was hope at least. After the news I had received in just the last two hours, it was hope I would take and hold on to. I thanked the nurse for taking the time to teach me how to use the straight catheter but mainly for giving me her time and knowledge. I was smart enough to know that my situation was not good. I don't remember her name, but I will always be thankful for her.

After learning how I was now going to have to pee, I lay back in the hospital bed and begged Keri to ask the doctors or nurses how my pain could be managed. I was not prepared for how the rest of the day would unfold. At about mid-morning, officers started to visit me in groups of three or four. It was so uplifting to see them, and I could see as we talked that my brush with death had affected them deeply as well. It had been several years since Officer Ron Munster had been nearly fatally stabbed while on duty, and this was a fresh reminder to all of us how dangerous a job we had. As I talked with them I found myself getting more and more exhausted. I loved their support and taking the time to come to see me. But it was taking a toll on me mentally in a way that I hadn't expected. As each group of officers walked into the room wearing the uniform I had put on for the last ten years, it was occurring to me that I no longer would be able to walk and run and do all the things I used to do as a cop. I pictured myself in a wheelchair as group after group of healthy officers came into the hospital room. It was starting to crush my soul.

I spent most of the next day in tremendous pain. I couldn't concentrate on anything because the pain was so overwhelming. It's hard to explain pain like this to someone who hasn't experienced it. First, there is the constant pain that won't go away and feels like someone is slowly twisting a knife inside you. Second, there are additional waves of over-the-top pain that just surge in certain parts of your body and feel like someone is punching you with a hammer. To me, it felt like I was getting shot again and again in my left side, through my midsection, and into my right hip and leg. What I didn't yet know is that the 7.62 mm bullet that had penetrated my left side was lodged in my right hip bone, surrounded by a cluster of nerves. Dr. Kozarski was unable to remove the bullet because of the risk it posed if he cut any of the nerves surrounding it. The plan was to see what, if any, recovery I made after a few months and then reevaluate the risk or benefit of a surgery.

After a week in the hospital I was damn-near pleading with the doctors and nurses for something to relieve the pain. When people were visiting my hospital room I put on a brave face, but behind the scenes I was becoming a miserable person to be around. I couldn't eat or sleep, and I was irritable. On top of that I was started on a physical therapy regimen. Because of muscle atrophy, physical therapists start working with patients as soon as possible. For me, it was too soon. It had been only a week since I was shot, and the therapy was extremely painful even though it was only range-of-motion (ROM) exercises in my hospital bed. In the middle of the night I was staring at the ceiling and couldn't stop tearing up from the pain. Keri had started sleeping at home again, and as I lay there all alone it was hard to focus on anything but the pain. I couldn't read or watch television without being distracted by the pain. It was becoming all consuming. I had had enough. I hit the button and requested a nurse or doctor. The nurse came in and refused to give me any more Vicodin as I had just taken a pill an hour before. I realized I wasn't getting anywhere and decided to take matters into my own hands.

When Keri came into my room shortly after eight o'clock later that morning, I asked her to get me clothes, shoes, and a wheelchair because I was leaving the hospital. She was not amused, but I wasn't kidding either. I told her that I could get more relief from my pain by drinking whiskey at home than by lying in the hospital and being given little pain medication. I hadn't thought through how I was going to use a wheelchair for the first time, but that wasn't the issue. I was serious because I couldn't take it anymore and hadn't slept more than an hour at a time for over a week. Imagine how it would feel to wake up from surgery in excruciating pain yet be unable to move from your bed. Then imagine not being able to relieve that pain. It was a living hell. Added to all this, every time I did close my eyes, I was often awoken in a nightmare in which I was in the shoot-out all over again. I slammed my fist down on the bed rail and with tears streaming down my face told Keri, "I can't do this. I can't take this shit anymore. If this is all that's left, I'm not gonna do this anymore."

As angry and frustrated as I was, I could see that Keri was scared. And why shouldn't she be? I had never looked so helpless and unsure of myself the entire time she had known me. She kept assuring me that things would get better, but that wasn't something I believed or wanted to hear either. I learned for the first time in my life what serious, chronic pain was and how debilitating it was psychologically. It felt like it would take a miracle to ever get a night's sleep again.

Somehow, Keri was able to persuade the doctors and pull off a miracle. Starting on my ninth day in the hospital, the doctors changed my medication to a fentanyl patch. The pain relief was noticeable and immediate. I was able to sleep, even with the nightmares. I was also able to interact with everyone—doctors, nurses, cops, and family—without a constant strained look on my face. I would never have recovered as well without this change in my medication.

There has been a lot of media attention on opioid abuse and overprescription. This is a huge problem today and needs to be addressed from many different angles. But this was not what occurred in my case. I know with certainty that I would not have been okay without the change and increase in my pain medication. I was already struggling with so many other changes to my body from the shooting that pain simply could not be one of them.

With my pain now at a manageable level, I was able to focus more on all of the other things which I had to grapple with, and two of them were major. First, the doctors had told me that they did not know if I had sufficient muscle tone in my anus to control my bowels. What devastating news. The hits just kept coming. Honestly, shitting in a diaper and having a colostomy bag were the type of things we talk about when discussing suicide. We would tell each other that if we ever found ourselves in that situation, it was time to check out. Of course, thousands of people lead perfectly good lives while dealing with these issues daily. But as I lay there in the hospital just short of two weeks from being completely healthy, these were blows I was not prepared to deal with.

To understand how devastating this news was, you really need to be a cop. Our whole career is built on a foundation of ego, confidence, and control. In every situation officers face each day, they must be in total control and aware of everything around them. They must do this bravely, calmly, and confidently. Police officers are the people you want to be with when the shit hits the fan. They will not panic but almost on autopilot will handle the situation just as they have thousands of others throughout their careers.

After a career of handling myself confidently and with courage, I was faced with a situation that I could not control. Not only could I not control it, it was humiliating. Having been a tough guy with an ego during my whole career, I was not equipped to cope with losing control over my bowels. It was one of my worst-case scenarios. Now that I could manage my pain sufficiently, I could not complain about my bowels. But I knew that incontinence was not something I had mentally come to grips with. Instead I just shoved it into the same backpack that I'd shoved everything else into all these years. Instinctively I knew that backpack was going to be a major issue for me.

The second major concern I was dealing with as the second week came to an end was where I would go after leaving the hospital. I had assumed that I was going home, of course, but this was not as simple as I'd thought. It was a matter I had ignored for the past two weeks, but this one was going to have to be reckoned with now that I was paralyzed. That meant a whole different level of care and rehabilitation than I was accustomed to. Without including me in the discussion, the city of Battle Creek in conjunction with the doctors had arranged to transfer me to an inpatient rehabilitation hospital for what they estimated would be a six- to nine-month stay. This was where I would both rehabilitate and live. I knew the rehab hospital they were sending me to, and the average age of the patients appeared to be about eighty. Had I been a part of the discussion I might have understood that because of my physical complications, it was in my best interests to go there. But I was really angry about the news and simply informed the representatives from the police department that when I was released from the hospital I would be going home. Period.

The same stubborn confidence that had defined my career was now coming into play and Keri knew it. I would be going home, whether I dragged my paralyzed ass there all by myself or not. She knew I wasn't going to go to the rehab hospital. Initially, the city of Battle Creek representative told me I did not have a choice and it was a condition of insurance coverage. I simply said that I wasn't going, that the city could refuse to pay for my care, and that I was sure that would look great fourteen days after its officer was shot in the line of duty. They of course knew it was an idle threat to make me go. But it was equally ridiculous for me not to consider the rehab facility because of the challenges that lay ahead of me. But I had not been a part of the decision-making process, and that rankled. I dug in. I told the representative that when the hospital stay was done, I was going to be sleeping at home.

I had good reason to feel this way. If any of you have spent even one night in a hospital, you know it is not a restful or comfortable experience. For starters, there is constant interruption and noise as doctors, nurses, orderlies, phlebotomists, radiologists, specialists, nutritionists, and janitors come into your room. And that is just during the night. During the day, you have all of that plus visits from friends and family. That family under the badge is a big one so I was not very rested even though my colleagues' visits were exactly what I needed. I looked at staying another nine months in a rehabilitation hospital as being as unrestful and stressful as the previous two weeks had been. I don't really know how much interruption there is in a rehabilitation hospital, but looking back on it years later I imagine it's quieter or else nobody would get any better.

Plans were made for me to go home. I had a hospital bed moved into our living room, because my home was so terribly laid out for a paralyzed person. There was only one floor on which I could live. To the city of Battle Creek's credit, once I had dug in and made up my mind, it made several accommodations to my home that aided me in the transition: from furniture to a wheelchair and having my rehab therapist come to the house.

14

CHANGES AND COPING

Coming home started with getting into a wheelchair. Despite the fentanyl, I was in excruciating pain when I got out of the hospital bed and into the wheelchair. I had been in a wheelchair only once in two weeks to get across the room and take a seated shower. Once I was in the wheelchair I had to learn how to use it, which was pretty simple. Except I had to take it a step further and learn how to do wheelies and balance myself on a tilt without falling backward. I actually got pretty good at it, as we had often sat in wheelchairs on night shift when we were at the hospital talking with nurses and doctors. Only five minutes in the chair and I fell over backward while doing a wheelie. I crashed and just lay there in the doorway to my room, looking up at the ceiling and smiling at my stupidity. But it wasn't the laughing matter I thought it was as I was still pretty beat up and the bones in my waist were healing. I found out later that I was nearly readmitted, but luckily I was released, this time with Keri gently pushing me through the hallway to the Lifecare Ambuvan for transport. I look back on my stay at the hospital with even more respect and admiration for the doctors and nurses who work so hard to make a patient's stay as good as possible under difficult circumstances. Thank you all!

As the Ambuvan pulled onto my quiet street, Wagon Wheel Lane, in Pennfield Township, I sat in the back in my wheelchair locked firmly in place. I was overcome with emotion as we pulled into the driveway of our house and I saw my car, the Saturn that I had driven to work two weeks ago. It took me a few minutes to process that and gather myself. Slowly the wheelchair was lowered from the van until we were finally on the driveway. Then bustling out the front door came little Jordan and Zachary. That made all of us cry as they climbed onto my wheelchair and gave me lots of hugs and kisses. It was incredible how much I missed them as they didn't get to come to the hospital as much as Keri did. We just sat in the driveway as the van pulled away. Zac of course had to figure out everything about how the wheelchair worked, and he wanted to go for a ride around the driveway. Jordy was more cautious, as I think the whole experience and changes in daddy were a bit scary for him. I knew he would have a lot of questions to ask me later, but for now he just watched me in the wheelchair.

When Keri wheeled me into the house, I was struck by the changes. Right in the middle of the living room was a fully reclining hospital bed, complete with a triangle bar hanging overhead to allow me to pull myself up and around when on the bed. The bed was facing the television, and alongside someone had moved the couch so I could see visitors. The whole room had been rearranged into a larger, more comfortable hospital room. The biggest change was still in progress. In the corner of the room had been a tiny bathroom that was not wheelchair accessible. The problem was already being solved.

Before my return home, officers had gotten together and torn out the tiny bathroom, completely reconstructed it, and built a brand-new one with a full walk-in shower. This is exactly the type of thing police officers do for each other, yet when you see this type of kindness being done for you it is amazing. Officers Brian Neil and Jim Martens, both accomplished home builders in their own right, headed up the project. Officer after officer donated an hour or two here and there to help Brian and Jim. The whole project took several days, and seeing all these officers helped me to acclimate to my new environment at home. I can't thank Brian, Jim, and all the rest for once again showing me another example of sacrifice and why I'm so proud to say I was a cop!

Not just police officers showed me tremendous support and love when I came home. I was really touched first of all by how my neighbors, led by Sheri Johnson, took up a collection. It meant so much to Keri and me to return to our home in Pennfield Township to find how much they all loved and cared for us. It isn't every neighborhood that is as close as this one was. I also remember all of the schoolkids and citizens who wrote me letters or sent me cards wishing me well. This support picks you up during some of the worst times. Keri filled the living-room walls with those cards and letters. I even remember one card from my class at Cooley Law School that had over a hundred signatures and notes on it. Again, thank you to all who wished me well and helped Keri and me through our transition.

The first night at home was challenging and more difficult than I would have admitted to anyone. I wasn't able to move anywhere easily, and once I was in the hospital bed I stayed there. It was easy to forget that it had been only two weeks since I was shot, and it would easily take over six for the shattered bones in my pelvis to heal. I was still incredibly sore, and it took me a good five minutes to transfer from the bed into the wheelchair.

So, I stayed put. Additionally, until the bathroom was done I could only use a bedpan. Interestingly, over the last couple of weeks I had dealt with the news that I might have trouble with bowel control by rarely eating. I hadn't even noticed it, but my weight had dropped over twenty pounds in two weeks. I could no longer ignore the fact that I might be incontinent for the rest of my life. This was the first of many changes.

I had of course discussed the issue of my bowels with the doctors before leaving the hospital, but I was in a state of denial. I lay there my first night home looking up at the ceiling of our living room. I hadn't really looked at it before, as the television was on or I was reading something. It needed a fresh coat of paint. My mind was jumping all over the place as I thought about how I had rarely slept apart from Keri, and here I was entering my third week without her by my side. She had decided to sleep on the couch next to me for the first night at least, but it wasn't the same. I also thought about the future and how daunting it was as a paraplegic. I had so much to learn and didn't feel mentally equipped to deal with any of it. I quickly shoved thoughts of the future to the back of my brain.

But it was hard not to think about my bowels, as ridiculous as that might sound. I was lying in bed wearing an adult diaper, because other than pain I couldn't feel anything. I could feel when I thought I might have to go, but I wasn't always sure, and there were accidents. The level of humiliation and shame that I felt was indescribable. An officer or two would be visiting me, and I'd have to cut the visit short because I had had an accident and could smell it. Each time this happened I was so ashamed that all I could think about was curling up in a ball in bed and hoping I would never wake up.

Over the next six months I started to shut myself off from the outside world. I closed the blinds and curtains, slept most of the day, and only interacted with people, such as physical or occupational therapists, when I had to. I was horrified at the physical obstacles I faced and didn't want to see anyone. This included friends and family. I quit calling people back and didn't really care if I talked to anyone ever again. I didn't see it, but I was falling into a dark hole of depression.

15

THE BLACK HOLE
OF DEPRESSION

Depression is difficult for me to write about. It is what I call the silent killer in law enforcement today. To understand depression, first you have to understand that it does exist. That was where I got into trouble in those first six months. At that time I had absolutely no use for the concept of psychology. Neither do most police officers. It has traditionally been culturally unacceptable for cops to show weakness, and the need to visit a psychologist while on the job has been seen as one of the biggest signs of weakness. Officers feel that a psychologist is someone they must see to get back on the job if they have a critical incident. They also view psychologists as people they must convince that they are okay, not as people who will help them. To be blunt, for cops, psychology is just an irritation that the risk management department will occasionally require so that they can get back to work. I wish I had known more about psychology when I was struggling to get back on my feet.

As I lay in bed with the covers pulled over my head, I felt like a dark cloud had formed and was hovering right above our house. I didn't want to interact with anyone and certainly didn't want to go anywhere. With her background in mental health, Keri was getting concerned. I just didn't understand what was happening. Those who have suffered from depression will understand when I say that it felt like a very heavy blanket was covering me completely and weighing me down so much that just getting out of bed was a major chore. I have never felt so completely alone and helpless. I think that was the scariest part of the depression: that I was helpless and not in control. I just kept sinking further and further into my bed, into what felt like a black hole.

The depression went on for several months. It didn't get better and only felt heavier and worse. It got so bad that I wouldn't even talk to Keri or the boys at all. I occasionally watched television in the middle of the night. I repeatedly canceled my rehabilitation appointments. I refused to return my own parents' phone calls and canceled any family visits. I began to hate everything about myself, who I now was physically and what I had become personality-wise. I started to think about suicide. I would just lie there curled up under the blankets, thinking about how I would do it. What would be the easiest way? Would I leave a note? Did I have all my affairs in order to take care of the family? Would I really go to hell?

I had expressed some of these thoughts to Keri. She told me she wanted to bring someone into the house to see me: a psychologist. She suggested Bill Heffernan, and although I respected Bill—a retired Battle Creek police officer—I told her there was no way in hell I was talking to a shrink. Keri persisted as my mood darkened. I told her if she brought a shrink into the house, I would kill myself. When she heard that, she took steps that ultimately saved my life. She first removed all my guns from the house. Well, all but one, which I had hidden in the laundry room on top of the furnace.

First, Keri had Bill Heffernan come in to see me. I remember Bill sitting on the side of my bed several nights for several hours. Sometimes he just watched a show with me, but he was there many times. I was in bad shape. I mostly refused to talk to him, so Bill started talking to me. He told me why he had gone back to school to get his master's degree in psychology. That he wanted to help cops understand that over the course of their careers, they were seeing some of the worst things a person could see. That they were forced to endure these things without the benefit of being able to process any of it. Bill called it a "backpack" that all officers carry. Because police are on the job for a long time, the backpack starts to fill up when we stuff our trauma and feelings inside. The backpack is different for each of us, but most officers, who view psychology and talking about their feelings as weaknesses, fill it up to the point where it's overflowing. He kept talking over several visits, telling me that we officers experience a very critical incident at some point in our career. In my case it was getting shot, nearly dying, and recovering as a paralytic.

Bill said that in the aftermath of this critical incident, officers are often forced to come face-to-face with their feelings: their fears and realization that they didn't have the control over their lives they thought they had, even for a short time. When this happens, whether by speaking to a psychologist or even a friend, something unexpected may happen. Bill said that the backpack officers carried might tip over, its contents pouring out all at once. This can be a breakthrough but is often a negative experience for officers. He said that all the horrible experiences officers have repressed their entire career cascade over them in an avalanche that could lead to severe depression. As their brains are forced to deal with years of trauma, and not just the incident that triggered the avalanche, officers may pull back and curl up in a ball, refusing to deal with anything again. But what I didn't know or understand was that a chemical imbalance occurs in people's brains when depression sets in, which affects how they react to all this. When police officers become severely depressed, as I was now, they need professional help.

Both Keri and Bill recognized that I was now severely depressed and decided to call a friend and psychiatrist, Dr. Sven Zethelius. Affectionately known by his colleagues as Dr. Z, he agreed to come to our house. I knew Dr. Z from some of the mental-health cases I had dealt with on the job, but I didn't really want to see him in my house. I was in a dark place, and when he first came over I told him I was fine and didn't need to see him. Like Bill, he was kind and patient and just talked to me for about an hour. Dr. Z was an experienced psychiatrist, had no problem diagnosing my severe depression, and prescribed antidepressants. He also told me he'd be back a couple of times a week and only asked that I try to talk with him as best I could. I found him very disarming, and I agreed to see him and take the medication.

During the weeks in which I initially saw Dr. Z and Bill Heffernan, I was still severely depressed. I can't reiterate enough how much I hated myself and what I had physically become in contrast to the mentally and physically strong police officer I used to be. It was at this time that a turning point happened in my life. I was determined not to feel depressed any longer. I was sure that all the psychologists or psychiatrists in the world could not fix what I had become inside and out, no matter how kind and understanding they were. I was determined to exercise the last bit of control that I had over my life. I knew where the gun was, and I got myself out of bed by flinging my legs to the ground.

This was not going to be easy. It was early in the morning so everyone was sleeping, but how was I going to get all the way down seven steps to the basement where the furnace was? Slowly dragging myself, that's how. And that's exactly what I did. I grabbed the carpet and pulled myself along, dragging my legs behind me. It hurt, but it wouldn't last much longer. When I got to the stairs I dragged myself face first carefully down each stair until I was in the basement. I continued crawling toward the furnace.

How was I going to get up? I saw the stepladder and set it up next to the furnace. I used my upper body to pull myself awkwardly up onto the ladder, enough that I could reach the back of the top of the furnace and find my .38 revolver. There it was, right where I'd hid it. I recovered the gun and slowly began the long crawl toward the stairs. Once I'd dragged myself back upstairs and into bed, I was bathed in sweat, as if I'd just worked out for hours.

Lying there, I put the gun next to me and let my heart rate slow down. I started thinking about everything that had happened over the last several months. The more I thought about it, the more the dark clouds returned.

16

FAITH

There is no more important chapter in this book to me than this one. Because I worked in law enforcement for many years, I know that many officers will hear "religion" and immediately shut down. Many officers find faith difficult because it deals with something they can't control or see. The concept of taking anything on faith is contrary to how police officers think in their world of facts and absolutes. I believe officers suffering from depression and committing suicide are subjects too important to have anyone shut down, so I ask that despite your perspective on religion, you read this chapter anyway.

For most of my life, my journey of faith was one that resembled a two-way mirror. When you look into a two-way mirror you see yourself. It's who you are on the surface: the clothes you wore that day, how you wore your hair, how you smile, and all the rest of what you portray to the world on the outside. On the inside, things are quite different for most police officers. What would people say if they knew what police were thinking at any given time? So, all of us are two-way mirrors to some degree.

However, many people wear their belief in God on their sleeves, both in the example they set in how they live their lives and in how they verbally profess their faith. For them as Christians, there is no two-way mirror. You get what you see, and they are witnesses for God. I was not this person when I was shot on September 25, 2000.

I was a raised in a Christian, God-fearing home. My parents took us to church twice on Sunday, and we all attended a Christian school. I was baptized as an infant and made a public profession of my faith when I was sixteen years old. On one side of the mirror I was a Christian who believed in God. And when I started out in law enforcement, I would have told you that I was a Christian too. I still attended church at the Battle Creek Christian Reformed Church during my early years as an officer. But something was missing. I just couldn't put my finger on it.

As I turned from rookie cop to veteran, I started attending church less and less. I didn't notice it at first because my excuses were outwardly valid ones. I was a third-shift cop and staying awake for a 10 a.m. service on Sunday was no easy task. I told myself I would just attend the service next week. However, if I'd truly wanted to go to church, I could have. I knew other officers working night shift who did. I was making excuses. I didn't realize it at the time, but during my whole life I'd just gone to church because I had to, not because I wanted to. When my life became more complicated it's no wonder that after about seven or eight years, I just quit going altogether. I didn't really miss it either, although every time Keri went with the boys I felt guilty. The person I had become was just not capable of opening up to something like faith and letting myself be vulnerable. It's exactly what I needed, though.

What was so complicated about my life? I was on a very successful track and had just made the rank of sergeant, and with almost a year of law school out of the way the sky was the limit. I can see the complications only in hindsight with the benefit of much reflection. That's the mystery of a two-way mirror. I was looking right at myself during those years and all I saw was success, ambition, the perfect life, and marriage. But behind the mirror stood my inside, and it was becoming broken and empty. The reasons why are not simple ones, but collectively they added up to a ticking time bomb.

I was approaching ten years on the job. In that time, I had seen acts of unspeakable evil, things I did not know existed in this world. It seemed one thing would always compete with the next as to which was worse. Eventually, cops become numb to these things and just handle the next one with indifference.

Later in my career, in the late 1990s, a mental-health term, *dissociative identity disorder (DID)*, was gaining traction. DID is defined as a disorder characterized by the presence of two or more distinct personality states. In law enforcement we were coming to understand that when people, often children, are victims of something so traumatic that their brains can't process it, they simply stuff this trauma into the recesses of their brain and deal with it by not dealing with it. Then later in people's lives, something would trigger the traumatic event that the victims had stuffed away. The victims would then be forced to confront the original trauma, which often manifested itself in an alternate personality. Through painstaking therapy the victims could resolve the traumas behind each personality and heal themselves again. I saw DID often in my careers as an officer and an assistant prosecutor.

To understand where I was after ten years on the job, I think of people who suffer from dissociative identity disorder. I had seen so many traumatic things. Each time I just tossed the incident into my backpack and moved on. I know this because to even admit to another cop that a traumatic event had bothered me would be an open sign of weakness, and such an acknowledgment simply wasn't done. It became easier to show bravado. Pretty soon, you viewed it as a game: who is the toughest on the outside? I knew I had repressed what I had seen and experienced on the streets. The more hardened and jaded I became, the less I was able to express emotion, particularly how I felt about something. About anything, actually. I am not equating this with the same type of dissociation that people suffering from DID experience. But the concept is the same. Officers just start to function on autopilot, and pretty soon their emotional armor is so thick no one can penetrate it. More backpack stuffing.

It is impossible for people to humble themselves before God when they can't emotionally open up to themselves or others. I was the furthest thing from a humble person on September 25, 2000. I had become a cynical, self-confident person who had left little room in his heart for God. In fact I started doubting how a God could let others suffer what I had seen. After all, why doesn't he just stop it? It's a fair question and one debated by Christians and non-Christians alike. God's answer was coming for me, but not in the way I would have expected.

I can still remember the taste of metal in my mouth from the barrel of the gun. It was just after two in the morning, and everyone was asleep upstairs. I kept my finger off the trigger, just as I had been trained to do my entire career. But I didn't remove the barrel either. I just kept it in my mouth, feeling very lonely and tired. I remember my thoughts drifting to how my whole life I'd been taught that suicide was a one-way ticket to hell. I pictured the devil on the other side, waiting for me in an eternity of fire as soon as I pulled the trigger. It had been just over six months since I had been shot, and I was paralyzed from the waist down. *Paralyzed from the waist down.* Just a few months ago I was competing in triathlons and starting to do well. I can still remember the feeling of running with the wind in my face, looking at my Ironman watch and challenging myself with each practice run. I remember the mountain-bike trails and endless obstacles each one posed as the bike cut through the trails in the woods. Tears began to well in my eyes as the realization sank back in that I would never mountain bike or run again. I was now a cripple for life, and I'd better accept it, or so I kept being told.

What scared me is how I didn't want to take the gun out of my mouth. I wanted the pain to be over. I felt this heavy cloud of hopelessness blanketing me. My thoughts flashed back to the shooting, and I wondered what I could have done differently. Nothing. Just thinking about the shooting made my side pulse with waves of pain, pain that the fentanyl couldn't dull. It was so quiet in the house that I could hear the clock ticking, ticking away time to which only a short while ago I looked so forward. But now, I couldn't even control my own bowels. Tears streamed down my face as I shifted the gun in my mouth. I just wanted all of this to be over.

My thoughts shifted to my family. To Keri and the boys, my mom and dad, my brothers and sister, my cousin JJ, my Canadian family, and all my brothers and sisters in blue. I knew that literally over a hundred people genuinely cared for me and would miss me if I were gone. Then the overwhelming feeling of hopelessness cascaded back over me. I knew I'd be a burden to all of these people, and they would be better off if I just weren't here. I moved my finger onto the edge of the trigger. As I lay in the bed my head faced the wall against which the television stood. It was dark in the room except for the sliver of light between the blinds that was hitting the wall.

As tears streamed down my face I had made up my mind to no longer be the burden I felt I was going to be. I had no reason to live as a cripple, and my life had been a good run. My finger was now on the trigger, off the trigger guard. Then I saw the pictures, the eight-by-ten-inch pictures of my sons, Jordan and Zachary. Jordan was three and Zachary was just two. They were both smiling. I stared at the pictures. What would my boys say? Were they even old enough to understand? What was I leaving to Keri? All these thoughts forced their way into my head. Again, the overwhelming feeling of hopelessness. I did not want to be a father who is nothing but a burden to his children. I'd be doing everyone a favor if I just pulled the trigger. I closed my eyes and resigned myself. I remember making sure the barrel was not pointed toward the top of my head so the bullet wouldn't exit toward where Keri and the boys were sleeping.

Where Keri and boys were sleeping? Oh my God, what the hell was I thinking? Keri was going to hear the shot, and I knew what she would find. I had been to so many suicide calls that I had lost count. Such an empty, lonely, and depressing feeling remained at the aftermath of any suicide. Those left behind always had so many questions, and they displayed a range of emotions from sadness to anger to confusion.

I wanted the pain to be over so badly. But I couldn't take my eyes off the pictures of the boys. I had never felt so alone in all my life. I took the gun out of my mouth, rested it on my chest, and cried for what seemed like hours.

Here I was, months after I was shot, lying in bed in the middle of the night feeling depressed and out of answers, with a gun in my hand. In tears, partly angry and partly exhausted, I prayed to God, "What do you want from me? Why didn't you just let me die in the yard on Parkway Drive?" I didn't hear a voice from the clouds or see any bright lights, but God spoke to me very clearly. It jolted me, scared me even, and I sat right up in bed. God told me, "I'm everything you want, and everything you need."

Then it hit me like a sledgehammer to the gut: here I was paralyzed from the waist down, an angry young man going one-on-one with God. I was directly questioning his plan for my life. I knew instinctively that despite my dire physical circumstances, I was in no position to question God. I knew by faith that God was very real, that this incredibly complex earth and all its inhabitants had not come about by two huge rocks colliding in outer space. I knew that everything that ever has been and is ever going to come was created by God. But most importantly at this moment in the middle of the night—as I shook my fist angrily—God was speaking directly to me.

So, God is telling me "I'm everything you want and everything you need." Lying there in the dark on the brink of committing suicide I came to realize a couple of things. I was not doing well managing things myself—that was apparent by the gun on my chest. And, I needed God's help. I had spent years ignoring and neglecting my relationship with God. What gave me the right to ask for his help now? Somewhere in the back of my mind I remembered that no matter what we have done in this life, God is a forgiving God if we come to him and humbly confess our sins. "I have so many sins to confess," was my first thought. I had nothing to lose. I moved the gun off my chest and set it on the nightstand next to me. Shaken to my core and at rock bottom, I decided to pray.

But, knowing God was speaking directly to me I was moved to pray in a way that I had never done before in my life—or at least not since I was a very little boy before bedtime. I dragged my lifeless legs off of the bed and with my arms lowered myself to the floor. It took some moving around, but bowing my head I folded my hands and prayed on my knees.

I prayed to God about a lot of things. I started with saying I was sorry for ignoring him. I asked for forgiveness for this and a lot of other stuff. I thanked him for saving my life, for saving it more than once. I then asked God to take my life and use it for his service. I told God that I didn't yet understand why he'd kept me alive, but I could accept that I am not God and do not understand everything. I asked him to guide me each day to do his will. It took a lot of effort to get back up onto the bed. I had lost a lot of upper-body strength and would need to work on that.

Just because I had heard God speak to me didn't mean the sun would rise the next day to a house filled with roses. I was still paralyzed and still in a lot of pain. I had a very uncertain future ahead of me. The next day I woke up wondering if I had imagined the whole thing about talking to God. But somehow I knew it was real. So I grabbed my Bible, a brand-new one that my mom and dad had bought for me in the hospital. I couldn't remember the last time I read the Bible. I didn't really even know where to begin. I asked God to help me out with that too. He simply told me, "Job."

Since I really didn't know where in the book of Job to begin, I just read the whole book. By the time I was done, I knew why God had directed me there. It was really an explanation for why I as an officer had turned away from God in the first place: how could a loving God let bad things happen to good people? Officers see child and elder abuse, and this question gets louder in their heads. The book of Job is as close to an answer as any of us will ever get while on this earth.

It is a story of a wealthy man named Job who had a good life and family. He didn't have any problems in his life, and he didn't want for anything. He was a devout believer in God. Satan saw this, came to God, and said that if Job had any hardships, he would certainly turn away from God. Over a series of tests his wealth was taken from him, his entire family was killed, and he was stricken with painful boils all over his body. Through it all he remained faithful, although he and his friends questioned God out loud, demanding to know why these horrible things were happening to him. Toward the end of the book, God answers Job from within a storm. In chapter 38:2–4, God says, "Who is this that darkens my counsel with words without knowledge? Brace yourself like a man; I will question you, and you shall answer me. Where were you when I laid the earth's foundation? Tell me, if you understand." God goes on in great detail over two chapters, asking Job one specific question after another, none of which Job can answer. Then in chapter 42:2–3 Job replies with the only answer he really could have given: "I know that you can do all things; no plan of yours can be thwarted. You asked, 'Who is this that darkens my counsel without knowledge?' Surely I spoke of things I did not understand, things too wonderful for me to know." Job repents for having questioned God, he is later restored to more wealth and family than he had before, and he lives a long life.

If you've ever doubted God about anything, reading the entire book of Job is worth your time. After I read it, I felt as if a veil had been lifted. All I had done for the past ten years of my police career was to ask again and again, "How could God allow something so horrible to happen? Why would he let it happen? Why do some of these things happen to some people and not to others?" But upon deeper reflection it occurred to me that I was very similar to Job. Before the shooting, my life was as good as Job's had been. I had enough money, had a wonderful family, and was in great health. Then I was shot and nearly killed. I'm not saying that there was this big discussion between Satan and God and that I was being tested. But what if, like Job, I was? How horribly I had failed. I had believed that I knew more than God did, when I knew very little. How could I even begin to know how to create an earth, make a human, or understand why things happen the way they do? All I know now for sure is there is a God who loves us so much he sent his only son to die for our sins and give us the opportunity for eternal life with him—and I'm not God. I wish I had all the answers, but that's just not going to happen here on earth. I'll save any inquisition for eternity.

My journey of faith has not been an easy one just because God and I are getting along again. I still have lots of physical problems and struggle with pain daily. But because I have put my faith in God first, it has made things much better and harder at the same time. On the one hand, my life is more blessed and rich than ever before, with the promise of eternal life waiting at the end. On the other hand, this is an evil and increasingly godless world, and shining the light of Christ in such darkness is harder all the time. I am not perfect and am still a sinner. The difference now is that I am no longer afraid to tell you what I believe despite all my imperfections. I know now that "I can do all things through Christ who gives me strength!" (Philippians 4:13).

17

THE CONUNDRUM OF PAIN VERSUS ADDICTION

Over the years since I was shot, there has been a growing storm in our nation and in the world, the storm of addiction to prescription pain medications. Every media source reports on this problem. Many stories start the same way: a back injury from a car accident or a work injury, then rehabilitation with prescribed pain medication, followed by either the inability to stop taking the medication as prescribed or an insurance company ending coverage, which leads the patient to seek illicit drugs. The drugs and addiction do not discriminate, as the victims cross all cultural and monetary lines in society.

My story is only a glimpse into what some people have experienced with addiction in their lives. For many, substance abuse has consumed decades of what was once a good life and made it a daily struggle to survive. I do not consider myself to be an addict. I believe that I went to the edge and peered down into an addict's hellish existence. Yet I was spared the struggle that is each waking moment of an addict's life, the struggle to find relief from the constant craving that drugs or alcohol has created in them.

I was prescribed the fentanyl patch only after my family and I had constantly pleaded for relief of my pain, pain that was so bad I was incapable of sleeping more than an hour at a time. I still believe that as potent a drug as fentanyl is, it was the right one for me to be taking at the time with the level of pain I was experiencing. I know with utter certainty that despite abuse of prescription drugs, these drugs are still necessary for legitimate pain medication in the treatment of traumatic injuries or other medical conditions. My fear is that because of opioid abuse, doctors will overreact and not treat serious pain like mine because of fear of being criticized. This is the conundrum of pain management versus the risk of addiction.

When I returned home, I was still wracked with pain. My body screamed out with what I called eye-watering pain, even if I simply shifted my torso in bed to use the bathroom or sit up. Now that I was taking a three-day fentanyl patch, I would feel little to no pain on day one, but by day three it was nearly unbearable. I remember staring at the clock on the wall and actually watching the seconds tick by into minutes, counting the time when I could get my next three-day patch. After taking fentanyl for almost two months, it was clear that all I could think about was getting my next patch. I quit eating everything except a few jelly beans, and my weight dropped another twenty-five pounds to around one hundred fifty pounds. I dreaded physical therapy, wanted only to curl up with a bag full of fentanyl patches, and leave the rest of the world outside.

This is how it begins for so many people. I initially needed fentanyl because I was in agony. But after about eight weeks my shattered bones had healed, I was getting around more in the house in my wheelchair, and I was beginning to use the actual bathroom more. This is a crucial point in pain management that is overlooked, in my opinion, and is the key to helping people relieve pain with opioids without getting them addicted. I had suffered serious trauma, but at about two months I was starting to significantly heal physically. However, because of my serious injury, I could keep taking pain medication as long as I told doctors and nurses that my pain was overwhelming. So by letting me drive the discussion of pain, the medical professionals were never going to stop me from taking fentanyl. About five months after my injury, I knew that my pain had gotten much better. It was still something we needed to treat with opioids. However, I had gone beyond needing fentanyl.

My need for fentanyl had gotten so bad that my body would soak up all of the drug in the three-day patch in the first day. I was starting to go into serious withdrawal on the third day and would curl up and start rocking, while alternating between sweating and chills. Something had to change. I admitted my tremendous need for fentanyl to my doctors. The problem was that eighteen years ago the power of these drugs was still not well known, even to experienced and educated doctors. Very little on this earth is as addictive as fentanyl. What I needed was to be medically withdrawn from it. Instead I was prescribed 40 mg of oxycodone six times daily. Thus began my first experience with full-blown withdrawal.

I was not weaned off fentanyl. It was cold turkey. I started taking the oxycodone, but it was not nearly enough to combat the fentanyl withdrawal symptoms. My withdrawal symptoms lasted all night and were worse than being shot. The symptoms started with profuse sweating for hours with alternating chills. I just rocked while curled up in a ball. Then came the cramps. My body had become so dehydrated that I was cramping horribly, and I wasn't drinking water because I had started to throw up anything that I had inside my stomach. I would alternate between rocking in place and trying to rub out a cramp. The pain from the cramps combined with the nerve pain I already had was agonizing. I screamed out all night long, generally profanity. Keri left me alone and let me go through it while she stayed upstairs with the kids. There was nothing she could have done. I did not sleep one minute that night. When dawn came, I was cramping so horribly that I needed to drink water no matter what so I started putting ice chips in my mouth. After about twenty-four hours I could start sipping Gatorade, but I still felt a strong compulsion to find fentanyl. Oxycodone didn't seem to be cutting it.

So I did what I thought I had to do. I found the bottle of oxycodone and took another 40 mg pill. After an hour I took another one. Finally, I found some relief from the fentanyl withdrawal symptoms. After drinking another gallon of Gatorade, I fell asleep. When I woke up I immediately craved more oxycodone and took what Keri thought was my second pill of the day when it was actually my fourth. I knew this couldn't last, though, as there are only so many pills in a bottle and days in a month. I resigned myself to taking the oxycodone as prescribed and coming up only a couple of pills short at the end of the month. Easily explainable. I felt like I'd finally turned a corner with the withdrawal, and after another uncomfortable day and night, I settled into a routine of taking 40 mg of oxy six times a day.

I didn't see it then, but I was taking a very strong dose of oxycodone and a large amount over the course of the day. Two hundred forty mg of Oxycodone is a lot for your liver to ingest and process in a given twenty-four-hour period. I also know that without a hospitalized medical withdrawal from oxycodone, I never could have gotten off fentanyl. I got into a routine over the next six months. My in-home therapist, Pete Vanderwiede, came over for an hour of physical therapy. Pete was a good friend from my church, and I always looked forward to seeing him. Then I saw an occupational therapist, Shawn Hoban, another good friend who helped me a lot with muscles cramping because of the physical therapy. I had a lot of scar tissue damage that both of them helped me work through as the months passed.

To anyone who has gone through a significant rehabilitation, you know the toll it takes on your body as you work so hard for the smallest gains. Despite dreading it, I gave everything I had to rehab, holding on to the slim hope that one day I might be able to walk again. I had relied on my wheelchair completely for the first five or six months, but I was hopeful because through a lot of hard work and effort my right leg was starting to show signs of life. I could slowly, very slowly move my right foot. That meant nerves were working all the way down the leg, and my therapists were hopeful that improvement could be achieved in these areas. Some doctors had told me that after about three or four months, when the trauma and swelling subsided, some improvement might occur. All I know is that every therapy session left me exhausted and wishing I had the strength to do more. I had spent most of my career working out, and I just wanted to get better. With rehab, though, it just doesn't work that easily that fast.

I kept taking oxycodone at the same dose but after about five months realized I wanted more and it just wasn't taking care of my pain. The truth is it was. I was sore and had significant nerve pain, but the high dose of oxycodone more than sufficiently took care of it. What I needed to be doing at this point was titrating off the medication by slowly reducing the strength of the oxycodone I was taking.

This is where I think patients and doctors are dropping the ball with prescription medications. Doctors just let the patient tell them how much pain they are in and don't really force a discussion with the patient. It's not all the doctor's fault. The patient is often the one being deceptive. But doctors need to at least push the need to titrate off opioids and figure out how much patients genuinely need for long-term use. What is happening with these strong opioids is that patients are turning into addicts. I was doing exactly this. Here I was on this huge amount of oxycodone. I didn't want to tell any doctor that my pain was lessening as the weeks of rehab passed. Instead I did what most people who have suffered serious injuries and are in my shoes did: I asked for stronger, more powerful medication. I asked for a return to fentanyl. Thankfully, my doctors refused. But they didn't slow down the amount of oxycodone I was taking either. I started to crave more.

As we entered the sixth month since the shooting, Keri had to hide the bottle of oxycodone because I was trying to take more than what was prescribed. On more than one occasion she had caught me taking a pill earlier than the four hours I was supposed to wait. Keri had seen addiction in the mental-health field and was getting concerned. I simply blew it off and lay in bed trying to figure out how I was going to get more. This is a turning point to which many people come when they are heavily addicted to prescription drugs. I was now there, and I was seriously contemplating a couple of things.

If I could have gotten in a car and driven, I would have gone to the places I knew in Battle Creek where drugs were sold off the streets and bought the oxycodone there. (Today many people today do this online.) I had no problem rationalizing this. I was a victim of a shooting and didn't "deserve" to be in pain. It just didn't seem illegal in my mind because the doctors just weren't doing enough to help me with my pain. All of this was wrong, of course, and buying oxycodone off the streets would have to wait until I was well enough to drive a car. Here I was a decorated police officer, planning on buying prescription drugs illegally on the street. Seeing these words on paper shocks me and is embarrassing to read. But at the time it seemed like a perfectly legitimate thing to do. That is what's scary about addiction—rationalization. The addict can see anything as normal and A-OK.

The second option was another which many addicts come to in the early stages of their addiction. I knew I wasn't going to put another police officer in the position of getting the drug for me. It just wasn't a line that I was willing to cross. Instead, I figured out a way I could cross the line myself. I knew that my family doctor, Mark Henry, had told me in the hospital to make an appointment after about six months of rehabilitation. I really didn't need to see him at this point, though, because I was seeing several specialists about my bone and nerve damage. However, I saw an opportunity and made the appointment. Keri drove me, and I told her on the way that I wanted to see Dr. Henry by myself. She was probably perplexed by this request as she had been in the room for all my appointments, but she respected it.

Dr. Henry has been my family doctor for over twenty years. He's not only a great doctor but a great guy too. We see him at soccer and baseball games sometimes as our kids crossed paths, and he's always friendly and willing to talk. When he walked in he had his usual semi-sarcastic smile and handshake. He always wore jeans and had a way of making things so down to earth. What makes him so good at his job is his ability to disarm you with his charm and get to the bottom of what's wrong with you. I knew right away that I couldn't lie to this man. So I went through with the appointment as if it were the normal thing to do. We both agreed to see each other in another six months and that my heavy dose of specialists was sufficient for now.

What Dr. Henry didn't know is that my plan had been to ask for a prescription for oxycodone for the pain. I would have had to lie to him and tell him that I was currently not taking a pain medication to get such a prescription from him. It also would have been a crime for me to do that, as it is illegal to knowingly get a prescription for the same medication from two different doctors without the other knowing about it. Once I had obtained the illegal prescription, I would have had to pay cash for it or the insurance company would have been alerted. The bottom line was that I couldn't lie to Dr. Henry. Maybe there was some redeeming quality in me yet. I felt tremendous guilt at even having thought up such a plan. Guilt: another trait of an addict.

I knew deep down that I was teetering on the edge of some-thing life changing, something bad. When I got home, I started imagining ways I could get my hands on more oxycodone. Finally, I resigned myself to the fact that I would have to plead with my prescribing doctor at St. Mary's Hospital to give me a stronger dose. I had an appointment scheduled as soon as possible.

When I met with my prescribing doctor, I immediately started telling him how much pain I was in. He was concerned that the high dosage I was on was not addressing my pain. I empathized with the position he was in. He is a leading neuro-surgeon at one of the best hospitals in Michigan and sees some of the worst spinal injuries possible. He therefore sees a full spectrum of pain-management issues, including nerve pain that is constant and requires lifetime treatment. When a patient is deceptive and tells him he is suffering from pain from a complex shooting injury that strong levels of oxycodone can't help, it's entirely feasible that this could be true. That's why I'm not being overly critical of doctors. I think my neurosurgeon saw the red flags but didn't push the envelope enough in the first six months regarding my pain management. He didn't increase my dose and didn't decrease it either. But in those first six months when I was becoming heavily reliant on oxycodone, I remember those biweekly appointments being only about five to ten minutes long. I was never really challenged on how my pain was from month to month other than what my pain number was. I always answered "Ten."

How should I have been challenged? I believe it's time we give doctors the ability to titrate medications by minuscule amounts, without the patient knowing. You mean lie to the patient? That is exactly what I'm suggesting, but only in the patient's best interests and only in such minor amounts that it would not be dangerous or threatening to the patient's health and safety. This type of solution has to become part of the discussion if we are going to effectively address the opioid addiction crisis facing our country today.

My request to increase the strength of my oxycodone should have been a red flag for possible addiction. When my doctor told me he was not increasing or decreasing the strength of my oxycodone, he could have reduced the dosage from 40 mg to perhaps 35 mg without my knowledge.

I realize this procedure may be impossible. The person or entity paying for the medication, in this case the city of Battle Creek, would only have to pay for a 35 mg prescription. For this idea to work, patients must get their scripts with 40 mg still written on the label of the bottle. Then, after the month is up, patients must see their doctors again and an evaluation must be carried out regarding the pain. The doctor would then look for signs that patients were complaining of a significant increase in pain.

If my complaints remained the same for several months, then perhaps a reduction to 30 mg could be made. It would be in patients' best interests to continue this blindfold until doctors believed the level of milligrams necessary to treat the patient's pain had plateaued sufficiently.

An additional suggestion that may aid in the legal issues surrounding such a deception: patients would be required to consent to their physician's deceptive titration of an opioid such as oxycodone if the physician felt it was in the patients' best interests.

Another alternative is the one used on me. My neurosurgeon felt my six-month visit was enough of a red flag for me to see a pain-management doctor. This was an excellent move, because after six months of heavy opioids, taking my next oxycodone was all I thought about. I had no idea how much of a hold the drug had over me until I saw this new doctor. I went into the office, along with Keri and my representative from the city of Battle Creek, who was monitoring my case. I filled out a lengthy questionnaire about the medications I was taking and for how long and about my shooting injury. When I went in to see him, I couldn't have imagined how the meeting would go. After he introduced himself, he sat on the edge of his desk and said, "Brandon, I'm going to level with you. You're an addict."

I was immediately angry. Nobody had ever used that word with me before. I knew what an addict was. I felt myself burning up as I sat in my wheelchair, my rage building. The doctor was still talking, but I didn't hear anything he was saying. He had called me what?!

Finally, I had had enough and cut the doctor off telling him, "You can fuck yourself!" He was taken aback by that and said, "Excuse me?" I again said, "You can go fuck yourself. I'm not an addict. I have arrested addicts my whole life and I'm not one of them. You have no idea what you're talking about!" He then tried to explain to me what an addict is and that I would need to have him manage my pain medication. He then threatened that he would be regulating my oxycodone use. I was so angry by this time as the words "addict, addict, addict" kept repeating themselves in my head that I told him the meeting was over and not to refill my oxycodone at all because I was done taking it. He was actually stunned by that, as he was probably more used to patients begging him for more. As I spun my chair and started wheeling out of the office he was fumbling for words and said, "It's not safe to just quit. You need to do this over time." As I left the office I said, "Fuck you! I'm not an addict and don't need your advice." And so ended my experience with a pain-management doctor.

On the way home I could tell Keri was not pleased with how that meeting had gone. She went on and on about how all the doctors were trying to do was to help me, and I didn't have to swear at him. It didn't matter. All I could hear was the word "addict." To me, addicts couldn't control their behavior. They preyed on others to support their habit. I decided right there in the car that I was done taking oxycodone. I am a very stubborn and determined person when I set my mind to something. I know much of this comes from a career in law enforcement. But I had no idea how stubborn I was until I decided to quit oxycodone cold turkey. Apparently at the level I was taking, it was dangerous to attempt quitting cold turkey. I wasn't looking at warnings on the bottle or researching it either. I simply asked Keri to stop at the Rite Aid pharmacy, where I bought a couple of bottles of Unisom, an over-the-counter sleep medicine, and a lot of Gatorade. I knew from my days on fentanyl what a detox physically felt like. I decided that I was going to sleep through mine. I had no idea how dangerous and reckless a plan this was.

I of course hadn't shared any of my plans with Keri. I saved that for when I got home. I simply told her that I was going to detox by resting my way through it and to keep the kids away because it was going to be a few days and it might get a little rough. That was putting it mildly. It would be one of the most violent things I've ever put my body through. I still remember it like it was yesterday.

I started out in bed sweating profusely, soaking my shirt and sheets. That was the first six hours. Then I started alternating between throwing up and diarrhea. I couldn't stay in bed because I was either soaking the sheets or soiling them. When I started to really crave oxycodone, when I started rocking while curled up in a ball of sweat, I took a couple of Unisoms. After a few hours I woke up in a haze and realized I had soiled myself. I abandoned my bed and just lay on the floor of the shower nude. It was just easier. If I was awake and overheating, I just let cold water cool me off. If I was getting the chills, I let hot water fall on me for a while. If I had soiled myself, I was already there to clean it. For two straight days I slept on the floor of the shower.

Every time I woke up in a haze, I felt something pulling me through it: a powerful craving to take oxycodone. I imagine this to be the hellishness of what an addict must go through every day. I have listened to many addicts in my job as they told me how they did not take drugs to get high, only so that they would not be sick. I understood now what they were saying. There is no way I could take that feeling while awake for long. If this was what an addict felt when in withdrawal, then I had more under-standing of why they would do anything—cheat, steal, lie—to get their hands on their drug to make them feel better.

As I lay on the floor of the shower, each time I was being pulled out of the haze I took another Unisom. Sometimes I took two or three because I just didn't want to feel the overpowering, craving grip that oxycodone had on my body. I have heard oxyco-done compared to heroin many times, as many oxy addicts turn to heroin when they can't find a pill. I woke up craving more. I needed to clean up with another shower. I repeated this for two straight days and nights: sleeping pill, craving, Gatorade, shower cleanup, cramps, Gatorade, sleeping pill. I had angrily forbidden Keri from involving anyone in helping with this process other than her. I don't know how angry I was, but Keri tells me she sent the kids to stay with family for the week, and it was just the two of us through it all. Another example of what I put her through, and how amazing a person and wife she is.

Somewhere around the start of the third day I started craving the oxy less when I woke up from the haze. I had nothing left in my system except whatever Gatorade I could keep down. I knew I was getting a little better when I drank three straight bottles and held them down for an hour. I stayed awake longer, took a shower, dressed, and went to bed. I didn't even need a sleeping pill; my body was so exhausted from what I'd put it through. I woke up almost twelve hours later, drank some water, and slept another twelve. On the fourth day I could feel the craving but compared it to how you'd feel if you wanted a cigarette really badly. It's strong, but not like when you want heroin. The craving lessened over the next few days. But I had another problem: I was in pain. A lot of it.

Again, the conundrum. How was I going to treat this level of pain? I thought about it and didn't have a clue so why not ask that expert I had yelled at a week ago? I set up another appointment with the pain-management doctor. He greeted me with a smile, and I shook his hand, telling him how sorry I was that I had yelled at him during the last visit. He asked me if I had reduced the amount of oxycodone I had been taking and if I was ready to begin titration off it. I told him I had quit cold turkey. He was genuinely stunned. I could see it on his face. He asked me if I had had any seizures. I didn't recall any so I said no, which surprised him. I explained how I had done it, and he literally had his mouth open. He just sat on the edge of his desk shaking his head and finally said, "You are the most stubborn guy I've ever treated!" After we talked some more, we discussed the pain that seemed to go all the way through my bones. It was so bad. We came up with a non-narcotic combination of medication that brought my pain down to a bearable level to this day. This stubborn son-of-a-bitch who wouldn't be called an addict has never looked back.

But I'm also more experienced with pain and know that when the human body is badly broken down, the levels of pain a person can feel are devastatingly infinite. I know that for many people, medication can be a tool to treat this pain. We need to continue the conversation about opioid abuse without believing that all these drugs are simply bad. They are not, and if you are unfortunate enough to feel the pain I did in that hospital room right after I was shot, you'll know it too.

18

FINDING MEANING
WITHIN PAIN

Many people will live their whole lives and never experience true physical or mental pain. Sure, they will break a bone or suffer the slow failing of our bodies as we age. This pain is real and part of the human condition. It is not my intention to minimize this pain. Life is hard, and the pain we suffer is a part of that. This includes the mental rigors of living in the daily grind. From raising a family, mortgages, car payments, medical bills, repairs on everything, and kids' clothes to trying to squeeze in a vacation and pay for it, and so on. And then the unexpected things enter our lives and pile onto our psyche even more: things like divorce, child injury, car accident, or death of a loved one. Each of us past the halfway point in our lives can attest to our own story of mental and physical pain.

But true physical and mental pain is not something all of us will see in our lives. I do not believe it is something you can prepare yourself for. I think it is something that reaches right into your soul and forces you to look into a mirror you didn't want to look into.

Somewhere around the beginning of the second month after my return home from the hospital I began to experience a level of pain that I had not felt before and did not know was possible. My pain meds were becoming increasingly ineffective as my body became used to them, and without taking more and then running out of my prescription early I was trying to adapt to the pain. I would stare at the clock and literally count the minutes until I could take another oxycodone pill. This was pain that was unrelenting throughout most of my body no matter what I did or how I lay or sit.

It was pain that forced me to either reach out for more help or retreat into a shell of myself. I chose the latter. It led to my severe depression over months as I shrunk further and further inside. I spoke to virtually nobody except occasionally Keri, and that was just in cryptic snippets of conversation. I just wasn't equipped to handle this level of pain. None of us is. Yet through it all I was able to discover what the select few of us who endure suffering at this level learn about the capacity for inner strength that a person has.

Despite isolating myself, I did talk once to a man with whom I'd shared many a long conversation about many topics as we drank coffee on night shift, my shift lieutenant, Mike Sherzer. Mike was one of those guys I'd describe as a "deep thinker" who often overanalyzed a situation and labored over the details of stuff about which none of us thought. He was both academically and streetwise a very smart guy, and I respected him greatly as a friend and coworker. I could not have endured without Mike's sharing with me Viktor E. Frankl's book *Man's Search for Meaning*.

Published by Beacon Press in 1959, *Man's Search for Meaning* chronicles Frankl's experiences surviving in German concentration camps. It offers a deeply profound look at the human experience in the gravest of circumstances, and I highly recommend it.

Sharing the book with me was vintage Sherzer. I had told Mike how much pain I was in and how there just wasn't any relief from it no matter what I did. I remember telling him how it came in waves, or just at night, but constantly, unyieldingly. A few days later he gave me an old copy of Frankl's book, which I have read many times since. I told Sherzer about this years later, but he doesn't even remember doing so. Yet it was just the type of thing he used to do when we'd talk. He was always referring me to some "deep thought" article after we had discussed one topic or another. He was always thinking like that, and on this day he may have saved my life. It might seem overly dramatic to say that sharing an old book saved my life, but I don't know if I could have gotten through my pain without it. There was so much to learn from it and from anyone who had endured the concentration camps in the Holocaust.

As I turned page after page in *Man's Search for Meaning* I was able to comprehend something I had never known: that some human beings suffered unimaginable physical pain for years and survived it. Up to the time of my shooting I could understand only brief pain. So here I was in pain that was mind-numbing, and I was reading about people who had been through the same. People who were shuffling through the madness of lack of food and drink and ultimately finding meaning? Was this possible?

One paragraph especially resonated in my mind and wouldn't leave it. While speaking of the suffering that he and his fellow prisoners endured, Mr. Frankl wrote:

> When a man finds that it is his destiny to suffer, he will have to accept his suffering as his task; his single and unique task. He will have to acknowledge the fact that even in suffering he is unique and alone in the universe. No one

can relieve him of his suffering or suffer in his place. His unique opportunity lies in the way in which he bears his burden. [Viktor Frankl, *Man's Search for Meaning*, Boston: Beacon Press, 1959]

The more I read it, the more I knew that I was going to have to make a choice. I was going to have to decide whether I wanted to make the endurance of my pain something that I accepted as my task or not.

I felt terribly alone carrying this burden of pain, even though instinctively I knew I was not the only one. There were others with similar burdens the world over. I also knew that I wasn't going to get any instant relief, nothing that would last any longer than a pain pill, and I was already taking the highest doses of those. What I knew I needed to do, what I would have to do to survive, would be to accept that my task was to suffer this pain and push through it. I needed to find the motivation that would allow me to want to live with this pain.

There was the hope that I wouldn't always be in this much pain. When you're in the worst constant pain you can suffer, it appears as if you can't see anything beyond the moment you are in right now. I thought of suicide all the time to relieve the pain. I also thought about the motivations not to do so, such as family, friends, and hope.

As I continued turning the pages of Mr. Frankl's book I was amazed at the levels of suffering that these amazing Holocaust prisoners endured over hours, days, months, years. Slowly a recurring thought began to emerge in the deep recesses of my pain: coming through this pain and emerging on top, albeit damaged physically, would allow me to help others and to tell the story of human perseverance over hardship. Maybe just as I had turned the pages of Mr. Frankl's book, others would find themselves feeling the desire to live and persevere. That they might return the cocked hammer of a gun to its safe position and choose life. If by sharing my struggles with pain I was able to help anyone out there, then passing it on would have been worth it. It'd be the least I could do after what Mike did for me.

Overcoming pain was not easy. It was a certain mental strength that led me past physical pain. I decided that if humans could suffer so greatly at Hitler's command and live to tell us about it, then it was my burden in life to at least try the same. I didn't believe my pain was anything like that endured by those in the camps. But because of what they had experienced I should be able to push each hour into the next, each day into a month. And slowly I did just that. I pushed mentally through dark storms and simply chose to live with pain. Eventually, I would take on the narcotic issue and pain as well. I discovered that each day you win over pain, you become stronger mentally. I refused to lose. And my reward? Life. Another day of life and all the precious mystery and blessings that it holds.

If you are suffering unimaginable pain today and feel there is no hope, if you are suffering beyond what you think you have the capacity for, I only ask you to consider what capacity a person has to deal with pain. You will have to accept it as your burden and try to find within it why God has chosen you to suffer. What part of the suffering is within the great design he has mapped out for your life? How can you find meaning in your suffering? Are you meant to be an example to others of perseverance through the storm? I cannot answer these questions for you. In fact, had you preached to me when I was suffering I would have told you to go to hell. All I can tell you is there is hope. I felt it that day when I turned the pages of that book Mike shared with me. I'm just passing it on.

19

"THREE THINGS"

The journey back from my shooting injury to where I am today is a long story that I could aptly describe as a roller coaster of ups and downs. I know that I could not be where I am today without the help of God and hundreds of other people in my life. I can't even begin to name everyone who contributed, whether knowingly or not, to my recovery. For example, I remember how early in my recovery my dad and brothers pushed my wheelchair around many NASCAR tracks just so I could go to the race with them. There are hundreds of examples like that in which friends and family helped me get to the next day. It is my goal today and for the rest of my days on this planet to try my best to pay it forward.

Once I had rid my body of oxycodone, it was as if a cloud in my brain had lifted and everything was much clearer. I often used the word "sharp" to describe how I felt. All the synapses that had been dulled were now firing, and I could start to formulate a plan for my future. My *future*. It was a good sign to even have any kind of thought about the future. It was such a struggle just to survive the past six months. I had shut so much out of my life that I hadn't given any thought to the next day ahead, let alone something as daunting as a future. As I put my faith in God, I moved forward, fighting to take that first physical step and with the confidence that I was meant for something better than just sitting and doing nothing.

Some very good things were happening in my life as I entered my seventh month of recovery. Through a lot of physical therapy my right leg was showing signs of mobility. I could move it up and down and was even starting to be able to put weight on it. I was using my wheelchair to move to the car and begin outpatient therapy. I was introduced to my new physical therapist, a guy I later called the "Gregarious Greek," Kosta Sevestopoulos. He is an amazing therapist with a true gift for getting people to engage in their therapy. I would not have made the strides in recovery that I did without him. Kosta pushed me every day through his mix of humor and work, and by buying into his motivation I was able to take incredible strides in a short amount of time.

By my eighth month post-shooting, with the help of a walker and crutches I could slowly move without the use of a wheelchair. For the first time it was becoming clear to me that I was not going to be paralyzed, and the realization of that fact alone was a very emotional one for me. I was confident that I was going to walk again, any way, any how. It was a tedious, slow process. Each step was deliberate. I still felt a lot of pain, especially after physical therapy. But now I also felt hope. I turned the same commitment and intensity that I used to apply to my triathlon training to rehab. I was focused and had to be slowed down by Kosta many times so I didn't hurt myself. With Kosta's knowledgeable assistance, entering month nine I could start moving around just using Lofstrand crutches.

Now that I was feeling hope, I started thinking about my life and future from a different perspective. I started looking at the big picture. I wanted back the three things that had been taken from me: First, I had been a sergeant working night shift. Second, I was in law school and working toward my law degree. Third, I was able to walk and move around on my own. Three thugs had stolen them from me in the blink of an eye. If I could get these things back, then I felt I could give the shooting suspects the middle finger and move on with my life.

I started with work. I never intended going back to work. I had been hit with so many things, physically and mentally, that working initially seemed like a ridiculous idea. Enter Chief Mike Olson. While I was in recovery, Chief Kruithoff had moved on to a job as chief of police in Ohio, and Mike Olson was moved from his position as the inspector of Internal Affairs into the chief's job in an acting capacity. Mike was a big guy with a bear's paw for a handshake and a huge smile to match. He already had a career in the Michigan State Police behind him, and he had been inspector for a couple of years. It was a hard job in which you investigated police misconduct and administered interdepartmental policy and procedures. It required that you uphold the standards of conduct necessary to maintain integrity within the department and community. In bigger departments it was called the "rat squad." Your fellow officers generally did not love you. Mike, however, took a different spin on the job, and when he came to see me at home I listened.

Mike asked me to take the job of acting inspector for at least a year, while the city of Battle Creek sorted out who would become its chief of police. My initial reaction was "Hell, no! I'm not coming back from a shooting injury to investigate officers' misconduct." But Mike looked at the office of inspector differently. He regarded the inspector job as the most important one in the police department. He said that if done right, the job wasn't so much investigating officer misconduct. Instead you were investigating how officers do their daily jobs and how their actions affected their relationship with the community they served. I still had reservations about it, but after listening to Mike I couldn't agree with him more.

I didn't have any set schedule, and Chief Olson had structured the job so that if I got tired, I just went home. If I could work all day, then I stayed. The first day back I think I made it an hour. But I had made it back to work. I had qualified with my gun on the range, an interesting experience to say the least, and was on the job again. I enjoyed working with Mike, but unfortunately he was not named the new chief and moved on to another police department. The incoming chief removed me from the acting inspector position and transferred me to the Training Division. Somewhere during this transition I decided that before I left the job I was going to return to the road and work night shift again.

Around the time I was in the Training Division, I reenrolled in law school and started attending night classes again. This was physically very exhausting, as I was not getting around very fast using Lofstrand crutches. Additionally, I still had to attend physical therapy, which thankfully I was able to do during my shift. I was determined, and after a couple of years, I finished my law degree at the Thomas M. Cooley Law School. I remember my graduation day and walking around the law school with my dad, who had also graduated from there. It was a proud moment for both of us and one I will never forget. I knew how much he had sacrificed to allow me to even go to college, and I was determined to one day do the same for my boys.

Around the time I graduated, I was determined to return to the night shift as a sergeant in the Patrol Division. There was pushback from city hall as I was still not able to move quickly. However, I could now walk with only the assistance of a cane. After a little lawyering regarding the Americans with Disabilities Act (ADA), I returned to the night-shift Patrol Division. It was an amazing moment and the culmination of a lot of determination to take back what had been taken from me. I knew that I had won, and that was enough to put the shooting behind me. I remember the first lineup with the troops when I returned, and it was one of the greatest nights of my life.

I worked the night shift for just under a year. In one incident most of the cops on the shift were looking for suspects after a shooting had occurred in the Washington Heights neighborhood. We had a dog track in place, and we received several calls as we worked the area looking for the shooters. At some point I found myself in one of the backyards and dispatch asked me for an update on our location. When I told them where I was, it hit me. I was standing in the backyard through which the suspects who had shot me on September 25, 2000, had fled as they ran to the van before we arrived. After we had completed the investigation that night, I couldn't stop thinking about how I had unknowingly found myself in the area where I had been shot. But that's how it is for cops. The streets don't change. Just the players. It's what makes leaving the job so hard.

Yet that night I had the overwhelming feeling that I needed to leave the job. That it was time. That I had put my wife and family through enough, certainly enough to not risk another shooting injury. I knew my career in police work was winding down, although it was earlier than I would have liked. That night, when I found myself again in the backyards of Parkway Drive, was my last one on the road. I can't tell you how much I miss it.

Officer 'back in the game' after shooting

TRACE CHRISTENSON
The Enquirer

Back in a patrol car, Battle Creek Police Sgt. Brandon Hultink first drove to the spot where he nearly died.

"I told myself that would be the first thing I did when I came back," Hultink said as the wipers swept snow from the windshield early Wednesday.

He pulled up across from the driveway at 431 Parkway Drive and recalled the details of each second before and after he was shot.

Minutes later, as he grasped the steering wheel and the car moved down Parkway Drive, Hultink, 32, had come full circle from the night of Sept. 25, 2000, when a bullet shattered his pelvis and strengthened his life.

"I'm glad I was shot," he said. "Now I have a great relationship with my wife and a personal relationship with Jesus Christ."

Hultink returned to work less than a year after the shooting but had been riding a department desk, first as inspector, conducting internal investigations, and then working in the training office.

But several weeks ago Hultink decided he wanted to work again as a patrol sergeant, the job he held the night he was shot.

He calls it "getting back in the game," but he wasn't sure it would ever happen.

Hultink had spent a routine shift on that September night, reviewing documents, checking on officers and even taking his dinner break at Arlene's Truck Stop before he and Sgt. Todd Madsen

Please see **RETURN**, 7A

Sgt. Brandon Hultink works the midnight shift Tuesday, running the shift line-up on his first night back on the road after a September 2000 shooting that nearly killed him.

TRACE CHRISTENSON/
THE ENQUIRER

Battle Creek Enquirer article regarding my return to work as a night shift Sergeant at BCPD (3/6/03).

20

THE BUDDY SYSTEM

S tatistics are all over the place regarding police officer suicide. However, on a national scale, "[m]ore cops die of suicide than are killed by gunfire and traffic accidents combined" (*Badge of Life, National Surveillance of Police Suicide Study*, 2016). We spend countless hours training physically to deal with dangerous suspects. But we don't want to acknowledge that we have any type of psychological issues for fear of showing weakness, even though more officers are dying by their own hand than by the dangers for which we train. And this statistic doesn't even account for the many suicides that are misclassified as "accidental deaths" to protect the officer's surviving family through life insurance or pension considerations.

For over ten years Heff told me that as a psychologist he was seeing hundreds of police officers a year. He said they were coming from as far away as Detroit and Chicago, mainly for fear that anyone in their department would find out they were seeking help. In 2018, as I write this book, I don't see that enough is changing in the way we perceive an officer who needs psychological help. It's a cultural barrier that will always be difficult to overcome. Heff and I talked about this often. Over a beer we would brainstorm on ways to approach this dilemma, ways that might help officers and lower the stigmatization that went with the mere mention of psychological need.

Most of our ideas were just rehashed ones, such as anonymously being able to see a psychologist, without the police department knowing. This was a good idea, but it worked only if the police department, and in particular the municipality funding the police department, set up a fund for prepaid treatment that also allowed the billing to be anonymous. Such a system wouldn't work if the cop sees a psychologist and then is later "outed" when the bill is sent back through. To the city of Battle Creek's credit, the municipality started just such a program with Heff leading the charge. It was called Helpnet and allowed officers, dispatchers, and any other city of Battle Creek employee to anonymously see a psychologist for treatment. This type of program is a good start for any department to address the stressors of the profession, and I encourage all municipalities that don't have such a program to set one up.

However, in my experiences working the street, I found that many officers still had no interest in even glancing at a program like Helpnet. Most officers do not believe in what they would call psychobabble. They just want to be left alone to do their jobs and would grace the door of a shrink only if they were forced to do so. I was one of these officers, and Heff and I both agreed that something more needed to be done.

I have lost many friends and coworkers to suicide over a twenty-five-year career. With each one of these suicides, whether at the funeral or in later discussions, so many questions are asked and statements made: Why would he do this? She just didn't act like anything was wrong. I talked to him just last week, and

I didn't know he was even having any problems. Why didn't she tell us she was suffering inside like this? I mean, we talked every day. It's heartbreaking to rehash all this after a suicide. But cops are analytical creatures, which creates perhaps the biggest dichotomy in law enforcement: veteran cops know everything about their communities and even their brothers and sisters in blue but know nothing about what's really going on inside themselves.

I remember my dad telling me something that I never forgot and for which I thank him today. Whether he intended it as advice, I don't know. He said, "Son, all anyone does at work is bring me their problems. If you want to be a leader, bring me your problem along with a solution." It's one of those things you just ruminate on later and realize how significant a statement it is. That statement alone changed a lot of who I became in my life.

When I have looked at the issue of officer suicide, I have often thought about a solution. It would have to be something simple, something that would be culturally acceptable within law-enforcement circles, something that would work. The anonymity of a program like Helpnet is significant and it works. It is the best way I've seen for officers and others involved in the criminal justice system to get psychological help and feel comfortable doing so. But still so many officers won't even look in the direction of getting help, let alone utilizing something like Helpnet. How can you get officers who don't want it get the help they need? I knew the answer was you don't. Then I had an idea.

While officers in crisis do not want or believe they need any help, what is it that they do their entire career? They help others. And who is it that they would give their own lives for at the drop of a hat? Their fellow officers. If you opened up to other officers and told them that you were feeling depressed, even suicidal, then I know your fellow officers would listen and then do anything in their power to help you. So, how could I tap into this ability to help others, while trying to help officers in need?

My idea came from a friend who was a longtime alcoholic. He had a sponsor, someone in whom he confided but who also held him accountable. That got me thinking about the culture of law enforcement. When officers are working on the job, especially those frontline officers on the streets, they have certain levels within their culture. Officers would give their lives for another cop. That's just the surface. Even if it concerns officers working in another city or state, cops wouldn't hesitate to take a bullet.

Then there are groups of officers who work together every day. They are the night shift or power shift or the specialized unit they are assigned to, such as an undercover assignment or detective bureau. In this level of law enforcement culture, officers are closer to this group of cops, with whom they spend most of their time. Within this group, the bond is closer, but officers still remain guarded regarding personal issues or problems.

Finally, all cops in the course of their career form a close friendship and bond with one or two people. I've noticed that even the most guarded and shy officers, ones whom nobody can seem to get to know, are still really close to at least one other person. It is this person to whom officers tell most things. *Most* things. But cops are still not telling this person that they may be feeling so down that they've thought about killing themselves. Police officers still fear cultural repercussions such as career suicide or being labeled as weak or unreliable.

I've thought about the buddy system. When I was a ten-year-old back at the Garfield Park public swimming pool in Grand Rapids, we always had to swim with a buddy. Even if we went to the pool alone, we couldn't swim without being assigned a buddy for us to watch and to watch us in the pool area. This was the buddy system. It was designed to assist the one lifeguard to safely monitor hundreds of swimmers and prevent drowning or serious accidents. The few psychologists out there represent the lifeguard. They can't even begin to help hundreds and thousands of police officers on their own.

The only people who can help identify a cop who is in crisis and suffering are cops themselves. Under the buddy system, officers would ask themselves who is the one person on the job I trust the most? This would be that person I have told or would tell my deepest secrets to. The person I meet up with to kill time. The person I'd call one of my best friends. It can be more than one person. Under the buddy system, I'm asking all law-enforcement officers to agree with this person that if they are having suicidal thoughts or feelings, they will call this buddy and tell him or her. That they would agree not to do anything on their own without talking to and meeting with this person at least once. I haven't suggested that officers feeling suicidal call a hotline or a loved one first. They're past the point of doing that anyway and likely don't trust many people. Often their personal lives are at the root of their problem.

The biggest problem with police suicides is that we don't see them coming. Often, it's a complete shock when cops kill themselves. These officers have told nobody anything. Yet all the while they have been suffering and declining inside. The buddy system at least attempts to address the initial problem. All we as officers have to do is to make a contract with ourselves to have one person whom we will call first if we feel so low that we want to end our lives. Some officers are so private that they will tell no one who this person is. Just so they agree to go to that officer when they need help. It is preferable if two officers, as buddies, make the agreement to hold each other accountable to tell each other if they feel suicidal. It would even be better if these buddies agree to simply talk more together about how the job makes them feel.

The buddy system comes out of the idea that many cops won't, at least initially, agree to talk to a psychologist. Instead I think they will only do what they've always done: talk to their friends at work. It's that important because officers are worth it.

A final suggestion. During my career, a hospital chaplain was always on hand to help the grieving parties in times of crisis and trauma. Many police departments are big enough to have a departmental chaplain. They have helped many people. Heff even started a program in which, after an officer-involved shooting, a group of experienced officers would come together to help the officers involved.

We need to destigmatize psychologists in the eyes of police officers by assimilating a psychologist right into the police department. This can be on a part-time basis for smaller departments and perhaps even full-time with an office for the larger ones. If it becomes socially acceptable within law enforcement, then it will be easier for officers to feel okay sitting down with a psychologist. I've found there is always at least one psychologist, and sometimes more, assigned within every jail. I think it's time police departments take a stand against police suicide with action. And it's not just going to address suicide. It will help officers deal with all the other things that pile up in their lives, and get stuffed into their backpacks.

21

REDEFINING
STRENGTH

I could write an entire book on the rehabilitation phase of my recovery alone. Those who go through a lengthy physical rehab such as mine need untapped mental and physical resources to make it through successfully. Sometimes the smallest gains seem to take forever and will come with many failures along the way. Failures that for me led to some amazing moments of change and some failures that were just that: failures.

We all deal with the physical issues associated with going to the bathroom. Until my injury, I'd honestly never given it a second thought. I'd lived thirty years and just taken it for granted that everything worked—until it didn't. When I was at the lowest point in my depression, I couldn't control my bowels. I would pray to God at night to not make me go through everything I was going through without the ability to control my bowels. Once again, God listened, but in his time and only after I had learned what he wanted me to learn.

When I returned to work at the Battle Creek Police Department, I did it wearing an adult diaper. I can't express how difficult it was for me to even type that sentence. I had to learn a level of humility that I had never before experienced. It's not that anyone could tell I was wearing one. But I knew. The doctors couldn't tell whether I'd recover any continence and tone in my sphincter. So it was either wear an adult diaper and go to work or stay home. This was one of the challenges I faced, and I chose the far more difficult path. There were accidents, and only close friends knew of my struggles. Through it all, though, I learned some life-changing lessons.

I learned that many people face much bigger trials and pain in their daily lives than I ever imagined. Things like cancer with chemotherapy. Things like full paralysis through injury or disease. Things my sheltered and selfish perspective had never contemplated. However, wearing an adult diaper for a year opened my eyes to a side of life that had always been there. I saw things in people's lives around me because I was no longer seeing things from the inside of a person who thought only of himself. Sure, I cared about helping people as a police officer. I just didn't really see those people. I started seeing people's suffering, especially of those close to me. The world slowed down. When each hour of each day is a challenge for you, you look closer at those around you and ask questions. Are they facing things as you are? Are they struggling with incontinence? I saw people with disabilities, suffering in every imaginable way. And then I saw something else.

I started noticing people who, through feats of incredible daily inner strength, were moving forward with their lives. They didn't quit. I saw a young teenager with leukemia going to school with a smile while still enduring rigorous treatments. Everywhere I went I saw people in wheelchairs pushing through their days, people I had never seen before. I saw the woman with cerebral palsy, striving to survive in a busy world that doesn't slow down. I saw for the first time in my life those who are depressed and trying just to put one foot in front of the other. I saw the unnoticed.

And then God's lesson became clear to me as if a dark, clouded veil had been lifted. I realized that everyone on this busy planet of ours suffers differently throughout life, but we all suffer. Trials come for all of us, and along with them a choice. Will we respond by fighting through the challenge or just give up? Simply put, we define for ourselves what inner strength means. For me, rehabilitation has taught me patience and perseverance in the face of failure. It has taught me to redefine what strength means.

I sank into a deep hole of depression and then with God's help made the decision to fight. I decided that no matter what path God had planned for me, I would do whatever I could physically and mentally to improve myself and my situation. If I couldn't walk, I would strive to walk. If I couldn't work, I would strive to work. I had a hundred little things going on in my life, but I decided to fight them all. I found an inner strength that only through my suffering could I see existed. For the first time in my life I saw how strength was not just muscular. And as he promised, God listened.

Against all of the doctor's predictions, I learned to walk again. It was not a fast process, but I rose up out of that wheelchair and over several years learned to walk with the help of a prosthetic aid on my left leg for my drop foot, a result of my paralysis. I learned to manage my pain without the use of narcotic medication. Despite the prognosis that my neurogenic bladder and bowel issues were not manageable, I regained my continence and have full bowel control today. I fought hard in the face of many physical and mental challenges. But this time, I did it with the knowledge that I was not alone. That I can't fight my way out of everything by lifting more weights. I learned that it's okay to ask for help. I redefined strength.

One of the strongest police officers I know is a Canadian, Rich Brouwer, with the Niagara Regional Police Force. He is a huge guy who was born strong. He's the kind of guy who just knocks you out with one punch and is the first one you hope you see when the bar brawl is on and you're the only cop on the scene. I go fishing at his cabin each year with close friends and family, and it is through him that I learned that cops are the same no matter what country they are in. It is also through Rich, a strong Christian man, that I learned there is much more to the job than physical strength. Through his experiences on the job I learned that most successful serious incidents in which he was involved were resolved through talking and verbal intervention rather than through physical strength. But until I was injured I still hadn't grasped what he, in his twenty-five-year career, was telling me.

Before my injury, I was in the weight room three or four days a week, coupled with a rigorous cardiovascular regimen. I was committed to physical fitness my entire career. Back then, if you had asked me to tell you how I defined strength, I would have kissed one of my biceps and laughingly asked you, "Have you seen my gun show?!" To me, strength was physical and the most important facet in my preparation as a police officer. This is nothing negative and should be encouraged. Okay, maybe not the gun show part, but the officer fitness issue. It could mean life or death. What I learned in my injury and recovery is that people don't know what strength really is until they face serious adversity.

Adversity comes in many forms: loss of a loved one, being physically abused, being shot and paralyzed on the job; the list is endless. And in these trials each of us faces, we redefine what strength is to us. Through these battles we go through, we discover how strong we really are.

A person close to me discovered later in her life that she had been physically abused when she was younger by somebody close to her whom she'd trusted and admired. This resulted in years of therapy and countless hours of working to put back together that which had been broken apart. Through this process, I witnessed strength in a person that I did not know was possible. I saw determination and fight in her that redefined for me how strong a person could be. It made me believe that no matter how horribly people are victimized, they can find light again through perseverance. I could not be prouder of her today.

Through my shooting incident, I too have learned to redefine what strength means in my life. From the moment I suddenly learned I was paralyzed, I had to make decisions. Would I lie down and quit or instead push through the darkness and clouds and move forward? Sometimes, this was just an hour at a time. Sometimes, I just had to decide to put one crutch in front of the other and make that one step. Many of these decisions were mental ones. Many were made with the assistance of professional help, such as from Heff and Dr. Z. Many were made with an arm around me from close family and my brothers and sisters in blue or brown. I learned that sometimes strength comes from allowing others to help you. This may have been my hardest lesson to learn as a police officer.

Each of us under the badge does such a difficult job. All are too important to each other to let anyone's inner suffering go unnoticed and ignored. We need to start looking out for each other more and getting each other's backs mentally the way we have done physically our whole careers. All of our backpacks are getting filled up. Some are stuffed and can't take anymore. Let's all have the strength to admit we need help. Let's as administrators applaud officers for showing this strength. Let's get to the point where such action is not only accepted but encouraged. Let's turn the page on officers suffering inside back to the point at which they feel they can tell someone how they are hurting, without hurting themselves or others.

I want to talk directly to my fellow officers who are hurting inside right now. I am talking to you as someone who has been right on the edge of taking my his life. I know the feeling of absolute despair and the dark, heavy clouds that come with it. I did not think I had any other options. I did not believe that there was any reason for a future. I believed that it was better if I were not on this earth and that I would be a burden to others if I lived. I thought I was going to be doing others a favor by ending my own life. How wrong I was.

On November 20, 2002, Keri and I welcomed Cody Jason Hultink into the world. We affectionately call him our miracle child. Cody has been an amazing addition to our family and is an amazing young man today. Had I pulled the trigger that night, he would not be here. Cody is my best example of how no matter how much you are hurting right now, or how much despair you have in your life, there is so much more for you in the days that are ahead. I know that in your pain all you can see is what's happening right now. As you are in those darkest moments, I ask you to do this: think about those you love the absolute most in your life. No matter what your circumstances are, your loved ones need you now or they will need you later. Weddings, graduations, learning to ride a bike, throwing a baseball, or simply sitting and talking with you. You matter. Police officers' lives matter. Please pause in the darkness and think about how much you mean to those you love in good and bad times. I've been there. I know that it takes strength to push through the fog. But there is light and it is there for you too.

I found an inner strength that I know can be found only with the help of God in my life. I know now through all my despair and desperation that "I can do all things through Christ who strengthens me" (Philippians 4:13). I encourage you to turn to him with a simple prayer and ask for his help in your darkest hours. I know that he will not ignore you if you ask for his help. I pray each day for all in law enforcement who are hurting. I don't know your names and don't need to. But I pray for you just the same. I know the struggles you face and will face. I know that you sometimes feel there is nobody on your side. How wrong you are. Hundreds of thousands of us are out there in uniform who wouldn't hesitate to give our lives for you on the job. Let's start to get your back when you are hurting inside. You mean too much to each other not to.

One of my fondest times in law enforcement has been sharing a pint of Guinness at the local pub with Heff and telling our police war stories. Embellished or not, police stories are the best way to get a group of cops together, and there is nothing more cathartic and entertaining than one tale after another bellowed out to the group. Listen for a few hours, and you realize how special cops really are.

Toward the end of many of these pub gatherings, Heff would often raise his pint and in his deep bombastic voice give us all an Irish blessing. So raise a glass, and to all of you out there in uniform:

May the road rise up to meet you.
May the wind be always at your back.
May the sun shine warm upon your face;

the rains fall soft upon your fields.
And until we meet again,
May God hold you in the palm of his hand.

May God bless all of you out there and keep you safe. You are all in my prayers each day, and thank you for everything that you so bravely do.

Standing up for the first time on my own since I was shot—
still a little wobbly and hanging on to Keri! (Fall, 2000)

EPILOGUE

Since I left police work I've often been asked what I miss the most. The obvious answer for me might be running. That certainly is something I miss dearly. Because of the injury on the job, I can't experience that amazing feeling of air whipping against my face as I run through the woods. It's something I often find myself dreaming about. But every day, in every city across America, police officers gather for a few minutes for pre-shift briefings before they go out to their duty assignments. They are crammed into a room together to review important details within their departments and districts. I miss these briefings most. They aren't long, maybe five or ten minutes, if that.

During this time jokes are told and embellished stories shared as an umbrella of camaraderie descends over the room. It's a feeling like no other as the bond between those who carry a badge is an unspoken one. All the people in the room know that they may not come home. They know they may go out that very shift and lose their life doing a job they've done for years. You may like some people you work with more than others. You might not even like some coworkers at all. But you know you'd lay down your life in a second for the officer sitting in that briefing next to you, across from you. That is one of the most unique and special things about being a cop. It's what makes a cop in Detroit and a cop in Los Angeles have instant respect for each other when they meet. I miss that the most.

So, when you see cops eating donuts or sipping coffee, seemingly doing nothing in their car, think about all the things that might be going on inside them. What have they seen or experienced throughout their career or even their shift? There's so much more going on inside those cops than anyone could imagine, as they work one of the most difficult jobs a person can work. Ask yourself whether those cops sitting there will lay down their lives later that day, leaving their family behind? Or if they'll become permanently injured? Officers in thousands of briefing rooms across the world know the costs and gladly put their uniforms on. They do so for all of us, and I miss the feeling of being with them all in that crammed briefing room.

Each cop has a backpack. It's unseen, but it's there. Let's all remember that.

INDEX

Milliken, Ken, 103-104
missing person call, 51-53
Mitcavish, Jim, 22
Mulder, Kevin, 15
Mullen, Dennis, 65
Munster, Ron, 111
Muskegon Police Department, 19

Neighborhood Enforcement Team (NET), 38-44, 57-58; primary assignment, 39
Neil, Brian, 119
neurogenic bladder, 108-110, 173
New Year's Eve gunfire, 61-62
Newlands, Calvin, 39, 43, 58
Newman (Commander), 65
Niagara Regional Police Force, 174
911 dispatcher/calls, 23, 38, 40, 44, 97-99
NYPD Blue, 45

off-duty pistol shooting team, 32-35
Officer certification tests, 15
Olson, Mike, 90, 106, 161-162
opioids, 113-114, 140, 141, 148, 150-152; titrate off, 144, 147
oxycodone, 141, 142, 143, 144, 146, 149; withdrawal from, 149-151, 159

pain, 2, 102, 106-107, 109, 111-113, 117, 139-152; finding meaning within, 153-157; medication for, 2, 113-114, 139-153

pain-management doctor, 148-149, 151-152
parades, 39
Penning (Officer), 61
Philippians 4:13, 138, 177
Pierce, Grady, 39, 88
Pierce, Mark, 39
plainclothes assignments, 68
Planned Parenthood, 46-47
Pocahontas, 52
Police Academy, 13, 43, 45, 50
police shooting, 90-91
proactive policing, 28
prostitution, 39
protests, 46-47
psychiatrists, 54, 74, 75, 77, 78, 123; removing stigma regarding seeing, 166

race issues, 92
radio code names, 39-40
range-of-motion (ROM) exercises, 112
rape, 64, 66
Reagan, Nancy, 29
Reed, Phil, 90
Reed, Tom, 57-59
Reinstine, Randy, 82
Rivera, Esteban, 39
Rivera, Tom, 97, 99-100
Riverside Golf Course, 82-84
Robinson, Christine, 101
Robinson, Matt, 101
rookie cops, 21-25, 64, 130; fear and, 47; hazing, 22, 32-34; idealism, 27-35, 51;

ABOUT THE AUTHOR

A graduate of Western Michigan University and the Thomas M. Cooley Law School, Brandon S. Hultink served for fifteen years as an officer with the Battle Creek , Michigan, Police Department and for ten years as an assistant prosecutor with the Calhoun Country Prosecutor's Office. Hultink currently works as a parole agent for the Michigan Department of Corrections. He lives in Battle Creek with his wife and three sons. *The Backpack* is his first book.

Real Cops on Cop Life

$14.95
Paperback

400 Things Cops Know

Street-Smart Lessons from a Veteran Patrolman

by Adam Plantinga

Written by a veteran police sergeant, *400 Things Cops Know* takes you into a cop's life of danger, frustration, occasional triumph, and plenty of grindingly hard work. In a laconic, no-nonsense, dryly humorous style, Plantinga tells what he's learned from 13 years as a patrolman, from the everyday to the exotic. Sometimes heartbreaking, sometimes hilarious, this is an eye-opening revelation of life on the beat.

$16.95
Paperback

Police Craft

What Cops Know About Crime, Community and Violence

by Adam Plantinga

Veteran police officer Adam Plantinga gives a thought-provoking and revelatory examination of policing in America in *Police Craft*. Writing with honesty, compassion and humor, Plantinga shows what the police officer's job looks like from the inside. Hard-boiled, sincere, and surprisingly funny, *Police Craft* will give every reader a greater respect for the police and greater understanding of the job they do.

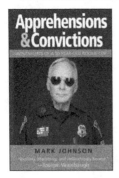

$18.95
Hardback

Apprehensions & Convictions

Adventures of a 50-Year-Old Rookie Cop

by Mark Johnson

At age 50, Mark Johnson wanted a career change. What he got as a new life of danger, violence, and stark moral choices. *Apprehensions & Convictions* is Johnson's explosive memoir of how he became the oldest rookie in the Mobile, Alabama, Police Department. In a crisp first-person narrative that is by turns action-packed and contemplative, Johnson writes frankly of the experiences, challenges, disillusionments and dangers that transformed him from an executive to a cop.

Available from bookstores, online bookstores, and
QuillDriverBooks.com, or by calling toll-free 1-800-345-4447.